ECONOMIC JUSTICE

ECONOMIC JUSTICE

The Social Ethics of U.S. Economic Policy

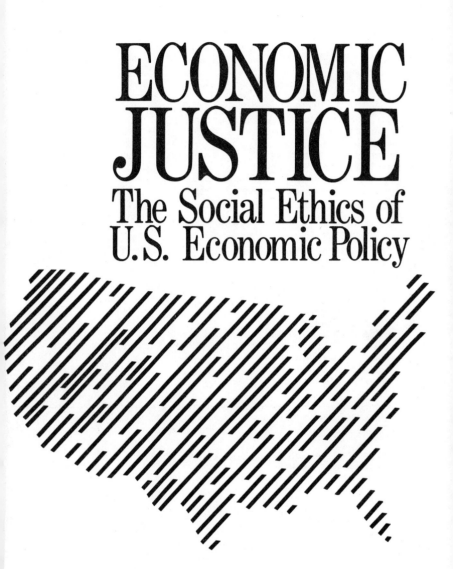

WARREN R. COPELAND

ABINGDON PRESS
NASHVILLE

Economic Justice:
The Social Ethics of U.S. Economic Policy

Copyright © 1988 by Abingdon Press

This book is printed on acid-free paper.

Library of Congress Cataloging-in-Publication Data

Copeland, Warren R.
    Economic justice : the social ethics of U.S. economic policy /
Warren R. Copeland.
      p. cm.
    Includes index.
    ISBN 0-687-11516-7 (pbk. : alk. paper)
    1. United States—Economic policy—1981—Moral and ethical aspects. 2.
Social justice. I. Title.
HC106.8.C666 1988   88-22648
338.973—dc19   CIP

Manufactured by the Parthenon Press at
Nashville, Tennessee, United States of America

To Clara Coolman Copeland,
who practices what I teach

Acknowledgments

This book is the product of four contexts. The first is Wittenberg University. I have tested these ideas with two or three hundred unsuspecting students. They have helped me think the ideas through and express them more clearly. I am grateful to Wittenberg's Faculty Research Fund Board for a grant in support of this project. I have discussed these matters often with Jeff Ankrom of the Wittenberg Economics Department, and he read the entire manuscript. James Huffman of the Wittenberg History Department read the proofs. Finally, Rosemarie Burley has been a patient and efficient typist at every stage of the process.

The second context is the Divinity School of the University of Chicago. Both as a Research Fellow in the Institute for the Advanced Study of Religion and as a participant in the Institute's Project on Religion in Public Life, my thinking was clarified and extended. In particular, I should mention two persons. I first did a close reading of economic materials with an eye to ethical principles under Franklin I. Gamwell during my graduate work at Chicago. I was lucky enough to share an office with Douglas Sturm, whose writings I was plundering at the time, while a Research Fellow at the Divinity School in 1984. For the interest and encouragement of each, I am deeply grateful.

The third context is the Social Ethics Seminar, a group of friends who read and respond to one another's work in progress. They read and responded to these ideas, and at a deeper level, the entire way I do ethics is rooted in this group of genuine colleagues. In particular, Roger Hatch has read the manuscript in different forms over the past three years, offering his necessary corrections and constant support.

Finally, there is my family. Quite appropriately, a small gift from the estate of my father, Rush Copeland, which was passed on to me by my stepmother, Delpha Copeland, helped finance my time in Chicago. My wife's parents, Florence and Robert Coolman, also always provided support. My children, Scott and Karen, suffered through adolescence while I worked on this book. Whether my absence was a plus or a minus I leave to them to decide. My wife, Clara, and I have come to realize increasingly the immense value of having a closest companion who believes in the work of the spouse as much as we believe in each other's. I am but an amateur kindergarten teacher; Clara lives social ethics. That helps more than words can say.

I deeply appreciate the consistent and intelligent interest in the manuscript shown by Davis Perkins of Abingdon Press. The editorial staff of Abingdon Press have helped greatly to put the manuscript in shape for publication. Of course, the work is finally my own, mistakes and all. I only hope it helps the reader think through this central issue in our public life with some greater insight.

Contents

Chapter One

Economic Policy and Ideology

There is a steel worker living somewhere in Pennsylvania who has decided the last two elections. We do not know his name, but we saw him interviewed by the media as he came out of the polling booth in 1980. He assured us he was a good Democrat and allowed that he did not like much of what Ronald Reagan said he would do if he got elected. Yet that steel worker reluctantly admitted that given the way things were going he just could not bring himself to vote for Carter again. When this same steel worker—at least he seemed to be the same one—was interviewed in 1984, he was equally apologetic. He said that he realized that the leaders of his union had worked hard to get Mondale nominated and that they were right about Reagan being bad for unions. He still claimed to be a good Democrat and a loyal member of his union. Nevertheless, he had decided that given the way things were going, he just had to vote for Reagan again. The way things were going. . . . Just what did that steel worker mean by those words?

Regardless of what they thought of Ronald Reagan or of

the specifics of his proposals in 1980, voters knew that the United States economy was not doing very well, and they believed that Jimmy Carter had little idea of what to do about it. Although they may have found Ronald Reagan's personality more attractive than the specifics of his program, at least he seemed to have a clear idea of what he wanted to do. In the midst of economic stagnation, decisiveness looked pretty good. In fact, the U.S. economy grew at about the same rate between 1981 and 1984 under Reagan as it had between 1977 and 1980 under Carter. However, Jimmy Carter made the mistake, or had the bad luck, of having the economy grow early in his term and stagnate at the end. On the other hand, Ronald Reagan managed, or was lucky enough, to get a major recession over with during the first half of his term. In 1982 this led to the highest unemployment rates and the lowest standing in the polls for a first-term president since the Great Depression. However, when the economy recovered just in time for the election, the result was nearly inevitable. Even if he had oozed charisma, Walter Mondale could not have changed that basic reality.

That the economy affects elections, especially presidential ones, is not a new discovery. No less savvy an observer of U.S. politics than Richard Nixon believes that the economy is the most decisive issue in our elections. He was convinced that he lost the 1960 election to John F. Kennedy because Eisenhower and his economic advisers refused to stimulate the economy out of a recession that reached its depths in the months before the election.[1] With that lesson clearly in mind, Nixon made sure the economy was heated up in preparation for the 1972 election. The resulting economic growth and the inept campaign of George McGovern made Watergate completely unnecessary. However, that overheating of the economy also contributed to the inflation of the following decade. Analysis shows that Richard Nixon was a typical politician in this regard.[2] It is a simple political fact of life that incumbents will do whatever they can to bring a growing economy to the polls with them.

12

However, the economy has been much more than just an electoral issue for Ronald Reagan. It has been the policy issue of his presidency. Certainly, there were many people who helped elect Ronald Reagan who had other agendas, abortion and school prayer for example. Initially, they were asked to wait until the economy was put in order. They are still waiting. First, the tax cut was the top domestic priority. Then cuts in domestic spending took precedence. When it became clear that the tax cuts had far outpaced the spending cuts, deficit reduction took over center stage. Even as late as 1987, Ronald Reagan's primary theme was an economic bill of rights. Throughout, the economy was the domestic issue.

At the same time, Ronald Reagan brought about a fundamental turn in domestic social policy. In the name of getting the economy moving again, he has created a deficit that threatens all programs aimed at basic human needs. The advocates of such programs are reduced to a fight for mere survival. Certainly, no serious politician can now propose any new initiatives in social policy. Poverty may have risen, the minority underclass may be falling even further behind, and the awareness of the dangers of acid rain may be growing, but there simply is no money available at the national level for addressing these and other problems. Rightly or wrongly, the issue of the economy dominates our policy debates.

So politicians think the economy is the key issue in the minds of voters, and (in the absence of war) voter behavior bears out this perception. Furthermore, once elected our politicians have spent at least the last decade focused on the economy as the central domestic policy issue. Voters and politicians have been wrong before. Yet in this case the harsh realities of our social order bear them out. Choose nearly any significant issue—poverty, racism, sexism, war, the environment, or world hunger—and in each case the issue is deeply entangled with the health of the U.S. economy. The number of people officially defined as poor goes up or down almost

13

directly in relation to gross national product (GNP) figures. Precisely because the major civil rights organizations realize that the most critical issue facing blacks in the United States is a black underclass which is left out of the economic mainstream, they are accused of forsaking civil rights for politics and economics. Despite the symbolic breakthroughs of some women into the world of men, women's pay remains far behind men's and efforts to establish comparable worth are attacked as alien to a capitalist economy. To reduce acid rain would cost money. The arms race creates jobs. United States farmers are awash in surpluses while Africans starve because our political and economic system has no way of matching needs to productive capacity.

In each case, economic policy at least overlaps with these other issues in major ways. To be clear, I am not arguing that economic policy is the issue upon which all else depends. Discussions about which of the critical issues is most significant are pointless at best and debilitating at worst. All are important, and all impinge on one another. It is sufficient to recognize that how economies are organized and how well they perform has become a fundamental public issue at least since the industrial revolution.

What Is New

Yet there is something very different about the U.S. economy these days. In Pennsylvania, a Lutheran pastor was defrocked for leading a disruptive campaign in support of steel workers whose jobs have disappeared. The United States Catholic bishops have felt the need to prepare a pastoral letter on the economy because it is raising human and moral questions Christians cannot ignore. Bruce Springsteen has emerged as a phenomenal success in our popular culture after singing songs about towns where factories close. Congress has threatened to punish those nations who contribute most to our massive trade deficit.

Books on the Japanese style of business management have become big sellers. Pessimists sound the cry of economic decline as our basic industries find it difficult to compete in the world market. Optimists celebrate the arrival of the service economy where the clean work of finance, insurance, and computers replaces the dirty work of steel, auto, rubber, and glass. What both the optimists and the pessimists agree about is that there is a transition going on in both the global and domestic economies.

Analysts as disparate as conservative Milton Friedman, liberal Lester Thurow, and socialist Michael Harrington agree there is something afoot. For Friedman, the reason for slowing economic growth and declining productivity is too much government: "Sooner or later—and perhaps sooner than most of us expect—an ever bigger government would destroy both the prosperity that we owe to the free market and the human freedom proclaimed so eloquently in the Declaration of Independence."[3] He believes we have reached a crucial stage where we must choose between freedom and more government. Lester Thurow identifies the problem very differently: "If present trends continue, America's standard of living will fall relative to those of the world's new industrial leaders, and it will become simply another country—Egypt, Greece, Rome, Portugal, Spain, England— that once led the world economically but no longer does."[4] He believes that if we do not act the United States will slowly but surely decline. Finally, Michael Harrington contends that we face a crisis: "America has entered a decade of decision. . . . The structural contradictions of this society are no longer the speculative province of futurists, philosophers and radical social critics. They are the immediate problems of policy makers and people in the streets."[5] These three disagree at least as much about what to do in the present situation. What they agree about is that this is a time of profound transition. New economic and political realities are present and possible.

Ideology Is Back

The election of Ronald Reagan not only brought the economy to the center of our political stage, it also marked the reemergence of genuine ideological debate. Indeed it may well be that the main reason Ronald Reagan was elected President was because he had an identifiable ideology compared to Jimmy Carter's. Public opinion polls tended to lump this in with the category of perceived leadership ability. As that steel worker in Pennsylvania might have put it: "Here is a man who knows what he stands for even if I am not sure I agree with him. What is it Carter believed in, anyway?" Surely Reagan's ideology was cleverly packaged, but, especially in relation to the economy, it was not all that ambiguous. He wanted less government and more market— fewer taxes, regulations, and social welfare programs and more of the magic of the free enterprise system.

This may have been obscured a bit by the rhetoric of supply-side economics, the political popularity of tax cuts, and the massive military building-up. However, even if interest, unemployment, and inflation rates were low, the budget more or less in balance and the Soviet bear in his cage, the Reagan administration would have wanted to cut social programs and taxes for ideological reasons. This was a central point of the famous David Stockman article in *Atlantic Monthly*, which created such a furor in the fall of 1981.[6] That some were surprised to read it in print can only mean that they had not heard, or did not believe, Reagan's public statements over the previous two decades.

Not all that long ago an ideologue such as Milton Friedman was considered intellectually interesting but politically irrelevant. A politician might steal an idea from Friedman's ever fertile mind, change it a bit, sanitize it with a politically acceptable name, and then propose it as his or her own. Richard Nixon did this with Friedman's negative income tax, giving birth to the Family Assistance Plan. However, only admitted right wingers would mouth Friedman's whole

16

philosophical outlook. Not now! Ronald Reagan compromised with political realities when he had to, but his ideology remained the most distinct and most consistently stated of any recent U.S. president.

Some see this as the inevitable swing of the political pendulum. After all, the liberals were in charge for so long that the conservatives had plenty of time in the political wilderness to get their thoughts together. For some time now any bookshop's shelves displayed graphically that conservatives were thinking about their ideology while liberals were either silent or confused. That liberal confusion may have reached its political peak in Jimmy Carter, but there is little on our political horizon to suggest that it has cleared up in subsequent years.

Most practical politicians and academics who disagree with Reagan's reassertion of free market capitalist ideology seem to believe that it is best not to respond too directly to it. Certainly few politicians running for national office now claim for themselves the banner of liberalism. Economic and political writers focus on the new realities of the global economy or the pros and cons of industrial policies as though they were primarily technical matters. When forced to admit a unified position of their own, these writers generally claim to be "neo" something—conservative, liberal, progressive, or whatever. Even social ethicists writing in this area recently have sought to focus on problems rather than ideological positions.[7] As an electoral strategy, emphasizing specific programs rather than general labels may make sense. As serious dialogue on political economy or as ethics such an attempt to escape from ideology leads to confusion and shallowness.

One basic thesis of this work is that it is impossible to escape ideology if we are to take seriously the full meaning of debates over economic policy. Instead of trying to ignore, or at least downplay, ideology, we should recognize its importance, analyze its ethical content and reason our way through to some constructive ideological views of our own.

The alternative is to find ideology continually lying beneath the surface of disagreements apparently about the facts. A second more specific thesis is that the traditional ideological options provide much better benchmarks for examining value assumptions than all of the neo-ideologies that have been put forth in recent years. While new economic realities have emerged, the basic options for fundamental assumptions about how a political economy should be organized are perennial. As we shall see this does not mean that we must simply choose among the same old options. It does mean that we must understand those traditional options in their complexity and integrity as a step toward constructing our own position.

The Value and Danger of Ideology

Our present ambiguity about ideological thinking arises not just from the confusion of the times but also rests in the very nature of ideology. An ideology is a coherent structure of assumptions about how economic, social, and political institutions interact and when this interaction retards and when it advances human meaning. Ideologies influence both how we describe what social reality is and how we prescribe what we think society should be. Indeed ideologies lead to different descriptions of the same events. An increase in gasoline prices can be described as freeing up the market, creating greater inequities, or illustrating the power of oil companies depending on the viewer's structure of assumptions. Similarly, ideologies suggest, if not dictate, quite different paths of action. Elimination of government controls, some system of industrial planning, or public ownership are all possible prescriptions for dealing with declining industrial productivity given different structures of assumption. In every case ideology shapes perception in critical ways.

Ideology carries both positive and negative connotations. Positively, it suggests a certain depth of thought about the

18

interrelation of economic, political, social, and cultural phenomena—the capacity to see all of them from a coherent, integrated perspective. Surrounded as we are by single-issue thinking and pervasive inconsistency, it is refreshing to encounter someone who can place issues within a broader perspective and consider their full implications. This is one positive contribution of ideology. It provides a coherent analysis which makes sense of the multiplicity of specific issues and which supplies some relatively stable assumptions about what should be done to deal with all these various specific issues.

Yet there are also negative connotations of ideology for most of us. All too often it seems that to have an ideological position is to have settled answers before hearing the questions. The ideological mind is too much the closed mind. Some ideologues seem destined to make the same speeches forever. New evidence, changed historical situation, or the opinions of others have no effect. For such people, ideology does not facilitate a more profound understanding of issues; it blocks serious grappling with them. They need not think; they need only apply their ideologies.

These positive and negative connotations are based in reality. Ideology is both inevitable and very dangerous. It is inevitable because we all bring assumptions to the consideration of policy options. The only questions are whether these assumptions are going to be conscious and coherent. If we are not conscious of ideological differences, we may assume that our differences are over data or interests, and that may be. However, clarity about our ideological assumptions should help identify just how much of our debate over data and interests is real, and how much flows from differing interpretations rooted in divergent assumptions. A coherent ideology makes consistent action possible. Such consistency is essential to ethics. When it is present, ethics can proceed to consider the adequacy of the grounds for action both internally and in the social context within which that action occurs. Random acts do not lend themselves to such analysis.

19

However, coherence is also important to religious ethics because it finally resides in some primordial valuation, some fundamental insight into what is important in experience. Using terms such as *ultimate concern* or *root metaphor*, modern theologians have recognized the fundamentally religious character of these primordial valuations. Seen in this light, ideologies are a sort of public theology, and (intentionally or not) advocates of ideologies are public theologians. Imbedded at the heart of their analyses of economic relationships and social forces are basic religious commitments about the character and value of life itself. It is this recognition that makes our task here theological as well as ethical. It also makes clear to those of us who take our own faith stance within a particular tradition, as I do within Christianity, that issues reaching to the very core of our particular faith are at stake in this matter.

There is also a danger inherent in ideological thinking, although it seems muted in this essentially non-ideological land of ours. Individuals who are the most extreme examples of this danger are unable to distinguish between their ideology and facts. Many economists in the United States lay out their theory of a free market, then proceed to assume that this theory explains how our economy operates. On the other hand, some Marxists still claim that historical necessities rather than human choices produce socialist revolutions. More common in intellectual circles these days are the relativists, who see ideology not as cold objectivity but rather as irresolvable subjectivity. For these people, facts have meaning only as they are interpreted, which is true, so they conclude there are no facts only interpretations, which is false. The dialectical relationship between facts and interpretation having been broken, untidy facts can no longer force the reconsideration or reformulation of an ideological position. Either by equating ideology with facts or by denying the existence of facts, ideologies become closed systems that cannot be challenged either on the basis of empirical reality or alternative structures of assumption. Then they are dangerous.

We are greatly tempted to try to ignore ideological differences. Do not bore me with all those old sterile debates; just tell me what is actually happening in this new economic world of ours. Yet as soon as we try to respond to that request, we run into very different answers. If we examine those differences deeply, we soon discover that the various answers flow from different assumptions. Inasmuch as these specific assumptions are a part of coherent structures of assumptions, we are back into ideology. There is no escape short of naiveté or confusion.

Instead of trying to escape ideology, we shall try to work our way through it in this volume. For the most part, this will not be an abstract effort. Rather, we shall examine some real live contemporary examples of basic ideological options—Milton Friedman, Lester Thurow, and Michael Harrington.[8] This will allow us to consider some very specific problems in present economic policy such as production, distribution, energy, inflation, and unemployment. Not only shall we learn a lot about what is going on economically, but also we shall come face to face with differences in both the descriptions of the economy and the prescriptions for policy. We shall trace these interpretive differences to basic value orientations and in each case shall be careful to be clear about just how these value orientations shape concrete perceptions. This will raise fundamental religious questions and require of us some constructive theological inquiry into the meaning and purpose of life. We shall then be ready to reflect upon the adequacy of the various value orientations and assemble an ideological perspective of our own. Let us first examine some contemporary ideological options better.

Notes

1. Richard M. Nixon, *Six Crises* (Garden City, N.Y.: Doubleday, 1962), pp. 309-11.

2. Edward R. Tufte, *Political Control of the Economy* (Princeton, N.J.: Princeton University Press, 1978) discusses the relation between the economy and presidential electoral politics.

3. Milton and Rose Friedman, *Free to Choose* (New York: Harcourt Brace Jovanovich, 1979), p. xx.

4. Lester C. Thurow, *The Zero-Sum Solution* (New York: Simon and Schuster, 1985), p. 47. All excerpts from *The Zero-Sum Solution* printed in this book are copyright © 1985 by Lester C. Thurow. Reprinted by permission of Simon & Schuster Inc.

5. Michael Harrington, *Decade of Decision* (New York: Simon and Schuster, 1980), p. 11. All excerpts from *Decade of Decision* printed in this book are copyright © 1980 by Michael Harrington. Reprinted by permission of Simon & Schuster Inc.

6. William Greider, "The Education of David Stockman," *The Atlantic Monthly* (December 1981), pp. 27-54. Stockman's own version of the Reagan gospel is described on pages 29 and 30.

7. For instance, Philip Wogaman has written more about economics than any other religious ethicist in the United States. His *Great Economic Debate* (Philadelphia: Westminster, 1977) was an analysis of ideological alternatives while his *Economics and Ethics* (Philadelphia: Fortress Press, 1986) seeks to move directly to basic economic problems.

8. Within recent philosophical discussions, Friedman's position is represented by Robert Nozick, Thurow's by John Rawls, and Harrington's by Michael Walzer. See Robert Nozick, *Anarchy, State and Utopia* (New York: Basic Books, 1974); John Rawls, *A Theory of Justice* (Cambridge: Harvard University Press, 1971); and Michael Walzer, *Spheres of Justice* (New York: Basic books, 1983).

Chapter Two

Liberty: Milton Friedman

Milton Friedman has led two lives. As an economist he is a highly respected student of the money supply, for which he received the Nobel Prize. As a political commentator, he was long seen as an interesting pure type, one of those benchmarks by which we locate ourselves, for example: "She is certainly not as conservative as Milton Friedman." While these two lives are not unrelated, as we shall see, Friedman has taken on greater significance in the conservative political climate of the '80s as a political commentator.

Friedman is a very interesting person, and his ideas deserve attention in their own right. However, our interest in examining his analysis is because he represents well one general ideological perspective. Examining a whole perspective in the detail necessary to make clear the connections between guiding principles and concrete analysis of specific economic issues is difficult. For that reason, we shall consider the specifics of Friedman's position. Then we shall want to think further about how he represents the basic approach developed in somewhat different ways by others.

What marks Friedman as an ideal type is his consistent and adamant advocacy of freedom as the only principle for public life. He stated this very clearly in *Capitalism and Freedom* in 1962: "As liberals, we take freedom of the individual, or perhaps the family, as our ultimate goal in judging social arrangements."[1] He has restated and applied this principle time and again since. Given the various meanings attributed to freedom, it is important to recognize that he means by it a very simple and limited thing—the absence of outside coercion. Since everyone is in favor of freedom, even though people mean such different things by it, I shall refer to Friedman's brand of freedom as liberty.

Friedman is convinced that generally people know better than anyone else what they should do. Therefore, people should be allowed to pursue their own interests, no matter how selfish or generous those interests, or how wisely or foolishly they pursue them. The goal of social policy is to minimize coercion, to allow as many people as possible to exercise their own interests as fully as possible. That is liberty.

The Free Market

However, we do live with other people. Moreover, for both economic and noneconomic reasons, we want to exchange various things with one another. This is no problem at all for liberty as long as these exchanges are voluntary, free of coercion. If we freely choose to enter into an exchange, it is an expression of our liberty, not a limit on it. This is a free market.

Friedman pictures such a free market as a collection of Robinson Crusoes who discover not only that there are others on their island, but also that various islanders have various specialties. While I am a good farmer, one of my neighbors is much better at making tools, another at sewing clothes, and so forth. Assuming I and my neighbors are rational about seeking what is best for ourselves and that we know good food, good tools, and good clothes when we see them, we can all be better off by entering into voluntary exchanges. The market is born, and if it is free, we all profit from the transactions.

Add money and the modern corporation and Friedman believes we have a description of the modern free-market economy accurate enough to guide policy. He knows that people are not always rational in seeking their self interest, but most are enough of the time that to assume all will be is fairly predictive of what actually happens. People are not always fully informed. More information is needed, but on matters that really make a difference to them most people educate themselves sufficiently. The greatest problem is coercion. Some of this coercion arises from the economic actors themselves if they are able to exercise monopoly power, but the greatest culprit is government, which invariably acts as a monopoly.

Limited Government

This raises Friedman's second basic commitment concerning social institutions alongside that of the free market—limited government. Friedman is not an anarchist. He believes that government has some essential functions, but they are few indeed. Specifically, he thinks government should (1) defend the nation from coercion from the outside and individuals from coercion from others on the inside, (2) facilitate the free market by establishing rules for exchange and providing the medium of exchange (money), and (3) respond to neighborhood effects and the need for paternalism. The first function, which justifies both national defense and the criminal justice system, follows quite clearly from his rejection of coercion. While the second function supports the free market, he would limit the rules to maximizing information, assuring that people freely enter into contracts, and seeing that those contracts are honored. As we shall see, he also projects a minimal role in managing the supply of

25

money. However, the third basic function easily troubles him the most.

Neighborhood effects are those cases where action by one person inevitably affects another—streets and sewers are positive examples and air pollution a negative one. Although Friedman admits that this is a place for government action, he tries to limit it even in this area in two ways. First, he believes that where the scope of a neighborhood effect can be controlled, those affected by it should pay the price, or receive the compensation for it. Thus, he is a great supporter of user fees. Let those who visit Yellowstone pay for its upkeep through entrance fees, not those citizens who have never been west of Cleveland. Whenever possible, let those who use an interstate highway pay for it, not those who do not own an automobile. He recognizes that this is probably impossible for city streets and neighborhood parks, but should be applied as widely as possible. Second, when the scope of neighborhood effects is so broad as to necessitate government intervention, free market incentives should be used as much as possible to deal with them. In line with this approach, he advocates graduated charges for pollution rather than direct regulation. Such charges create something like a market incentive to clean up the air and water. On the positive front, he recognizes that we all have a stake in an educated citizenry. However, he proposes that we respond to that neighborhood effect by providing parents with educational vouchers which they can spend at any school rather than through a monopolistic public school system. In sum, he limits the scope of what he considers neighborhood effects and tries to handle them in ways that are as consistent as possible with a free market.

He is even more careful about paternalism. In the final analysis, he believes government should protect only children and the mentally incompetent. Indeed, he believes that the most significant mistake we have made in recent years is to extend paternalism too broadly.

> Emphasis on the responsibility of the individual for his own fate was replaced by emphasis on the individual as a pawn buffeted by forces beyond his control. The view that government's role is to serve as an umpire to prevent individuals from coercing one another was replaced by the view that government's role is to serve as a parent charged with the duty of coercing some to aid others.[2]

In other words, he rejects programs based on paternalism because they force taxpayers to provide assistance against their will and because they usually limit the freedom of the recipient to act as he or she chooses. A major exception to this position is his advocacy of a negative income tax, cash assistance to the poor. In a complex society, we may want to provide charity through government channels. However, it should be kept clear that this is charity which can be withdrawn by majority vote at any time. It should be granted on the basis of income, eliminating bureaucratic determination of who should or should not work, who should or should not sleep together, and so forth. It should be in cash so recipients can spend it as they choose in the market. Once again, the scope of government is limited and what government action there is fits into the free market as much as possible.

Friedman wants to place limits on government essentially because governmental decisions are by their very nature authoritarian; they coerce. Democracy does not solve this problem since coercion by a majority still destroys liberty for the minority. Such authoritarianism, from whatever source, is the most troubling problem in organizing a society for a classical liberal such as Friedman. While there are other sources of authoritarianism in any society, according to Friedman none compare to government. The only solution is to keep government small, to limit its function to the primarily negative one of preventing coercion.

A word is needed about how the free market and limited government reinforce one another. It should be clear that the view of government advocated by Friedman supports the free market. It is limited in order to leave as much as possible to the market. Its primary function is to create the structure within which a market operates. Whatever else it does, to deal with neighborhood effects or to exercise paternalism, should be done in ways most consistent with the market.

A little less clear is how the free market makes limited government possible. The free market handles so many matters through voluntary exchange that we have little need for government. Friedman thinks we take this for granted. "By enabling people to cooperate with one another without coercion or central direction, it reduces the area over which political power is exercised."[3] Two other ways the free market supports not just limited but free government are (1) creating dispersed centers of economic power and (2) supporting dissent. Since Friedman fears governmental power most, he welcomes the development of centers of economic power that can counterbalance the power of government. He does not fear this economic power very much because he thinks the free market generates dispersed rather than centralized power. Finally, the free market makes it possible to raise funds for unpopular causes. Socialists can raise money to spread their ideas in a free-market economy. Capitalists can do the same under socialism only with great difficulty.

Friedman recognizes that it is possible to have authoritarian governments in nations where the economy operates primarily as a free market. The free market does not guarantee political freedom. However, he contends that political freedom is impossible for any length of time without a free market.

> Historical evidence speaks with a single voice on the relation between political freedom and a free market. I know of no example in time or place of a society that has been marked by a large measure of political freedom, and that has not also used something comparable to a free market to organize the bulk of economic activity.[4]

The free market may not be sufficient to guarantee political freedom, but it is necessary to make such freedom possible.

Both the free market and limited government are ultimately justified on the basis of maximizing individual liberty. Friedman believes the free market does this by allowing consumers to buy what they want as long as producers can supply it at a price they are willing to pay. The consumer and producer are free to enter into or reject the transaction. Producers compete for the business of the consumers, choices multiply, and liberty grows. Government can facilitate these transactions by preventing coercion and enforcing contracts. Limited government keeps government from restricting these choices unnecessarily by forcing people to act as government orders rather than as the people choose. If government is limited and the market allowed to operate, liberty thrives.

Productivity

Some will say that all of this is interesting social and political theory or ideology, but what about economics. Since this book is addressed to citizens rather than to economists, we shall not delve into the details of Friedman's calculations of the money supply. However, we do need to touch upon some of the broad outline of his economic theory in order to understand how he addresses some fairly typical contemporary problems in economic policy.

We have already seen how various Robinson Crusoes could improve their economic standing by trading. The result was a higher standard of living for each. This was possible because some were more productive than others, at least at their specialty. The result was an increase in overall productivity for our island. As long as I can grow more tomatoes in the time I save by not needing to make a hoe, than my neighbor wants in exchange for that hoe, I come out ahead. Of course, I have to know which of my neighbors is better at hoes than tomatoes. That might be possible on a

29

small island but not in a modern economy. For Friedman, this is where money and prices enter as a means of facilitating exchange.

Prices play three functions according to Friedman, two of which are related to efficiency or productivity. First, prices communicate information. They signal producers what consumers want and what they are willing to pay for it; they signal consumers what producers can make available and at what cost. Nicely, prices tell both producers and consumers only what they need to know to act. Lumberjacks in Oregon do not need to know whether prices are up because there is increased demand for houses in Japan, furniture produced in North Carolina, or pencils made in Mexico. If prices are up, someone somewhere wants more lumber, or many people in many places. That is all the lumberjacks need to know.

However, prices also reinforce this function of communicating information by playing the second function of providing incentives for people to respond to that information. To follow out our example, if the price of lumber goes up it becomes profitable for lumber companies to hire more workers or pay overtime to produce more wood in response to the signal of increased demand. Higher gasoline prices provide a comparable incentive to motorists to respond to the information that the supply of gasoline is down by driving less, buying a higher mileage auto, or giving up something else.

The overall result in a free market economy is competition among consumers to buy, and among producers to supply, the best possible product at the lowest possible price. This is the case not because of the goodwill of anyone, but because the market system allows consumers to reward those who provide what they want at the lowest price and to punish those who do not. There is, in other words, an inherent drive in a free market economy toward greater efficiency and greater productivity. There is no need for an overall plan for such efficiency to occur. Just get out of the way and allow the market to work. Indeed, for Friedman the failure of an economy to be productive indicates some interference in the free market by someone, most likely government.

As specific evidence for this theory, Friedman points to nations in which he believes free markets dominate—Hong Kong, Japan, and West Germany—contrasting them to nations where they do not—China, India, and East Germany. Alternatively, he contrasts Great Britain and the United States at the present time to the nineteenth century, when both were more market oriented. Throughout, he argues that the miracle of the market has produced dynamic economies marked by increasing productivity and general economic growth. Intervention in the market has led to rigidity and stagnation. Thus, Friedman offers no specific program for increased productivity. Rather, he contends that any policies which reduce government restrictions upon the market, freeing it up to work its magic, should lead to greater productivity. What is needed is not a government policy to facilitate productivity, but rather less government.

"The private-enterprise system is often described as a profit system. That is a misnomer. It is a profit and *loss* system. If anything, the loss part is even more vital than the profit part."[5] According to Friedman, stockholders and lenders make the basic judgments on who is to lose in our present economy. If, in the opinion of these people, an enterprise is in trouble only because of bad luck, they will continue to risk their money. If not, they will refuse. As usual, Friedman finds considerable value in this market reality: "That undoubtedly is harsh on some individuals as well as on some companies. But it is highly beneficial for the community as a whole because it assures that resources are directed toward those enterprises that will use them most effectively."[6]

Friedman is particularly adamant in rejecting proposals for an industrial policy in the United States, policies designed to assist industries to develop the capacity to compete. He says "The United States has had an industrial policy since its

31

beginning, and a very successful one indeed, identifiable as free markets, private property, and competition."[7] He sees no reason to change that policy. The likely result of an industrial policy in his view would be to add further rigidity to the economic system. By attempting to prop up declining industries it would prevent the natural movement of the market toward more productive enterprises. The result would be to hamstring the economic system that has worked too well in the past. He concludes: "This system produced the remarkable growth in the productivity of the U.S. economy during the past two centuries. Our increasing rejection of this system in favor of a government-controlled economy is a major reason why productivity in recent years has gone into reverse."[8]

Distribution

Besides communicating information and providing incentives, prices perform a third function according to Friedman. They distribute income. Moreover, they distribute income unequally. Those who produce more of what people will buy receive higher incomes; those who produce less of what sells get lower incomes. Friedman states the result in principle as, "To each according to what he and the instruments he owns produces."[9] This will not produce equality of results. Recognizing that this may seem unfair, Friedman defends it in principle and in practice. He has referred to this principle as equality of opportunity, which he defines in this way: "No arbitrary obstacles should prevent people from achieving those positions for which their talents fit them and which their values lead them to seek. Not birth, nationality, color, religion, sex, nor any other irrelevant characteristic should determine the opportunities that are open to a person—only his abilities."[10] It is this kind of equality which the free market allows and rewards according to Friedman.

In principle, he sees no way that equality is possible without restricting freedom. If we attempt to prevent difference in rewards in the first place, we shall have to forsake the price mechanism. This necessitates some other system for communicating information and providing incentives, some system established by authority. In other words, someone must tell us what to produce and what reward we shall receive for producing it. Liberty gives way to orders. If we attempt to redistribute the rewards after the price system has operated, we can only do so by limiting the freedom of persons to enjoy, pass on, or even give away what they have gained by being productive. Friedman finds no ethical grounds for adjudicating among the various principles of equality on their own terms. Judged on its contribution to the singular principle of liberty, equality of opportunity (reward for performance) is clearly superior.

Fortunately, as Friedman sees it, the results are not even so unequal in practice. Not only do all prosper from the productivity of the free market, but the resulting affluence improves the actual conditions of the masses more than the wealthy. This is because basic consumer goods are made generally available. "Modern plumbing, central heating, automobiles, television, radio, to cite just a few examples, provide conveniences to the masses equivalent to those that the wealthy could always get by the use of servants, entertainers and so on."[11] The result is that the masses live like the wealthy in traditional societies. While the upper-classes may have more, the more they have is relatively non-essential luxuries. In the necessities of life, there is actually a general equality in developed capitalist economies. Thus, while we may tolerate inequality in the name of liberty, the resulting efficiency leads to such productivity that everyone is better off, especially the poor.

But he admits that some remain in need and that out of our sympathy for them we want to help. Since most of us feel this way and society is so complex, government may be the best way to provide assistance. However, as I mentioned in discussing the role of government, Friedman wants to do this in a way which least disrupts the free market. Thus, he

33

opposes farm subsidies, minimum wage laws, social service programs, and the like and proposes instead a negative income tax. His negative income tax would provide a direct cash grant to people based on their income alone. People who work would only lose fifty cents of the grant for every dollar they earned, so they would still have an incentive to get a job and work for pay raises. The grant would be administered something like the Internal Revenue Service does with the personal income tax, eliminating the welfare bureaucracy. All other welfare programs would be eliminated. This would not end inequality of result. It would provide some cash to the very poor who could spend it in the marketplace as they chose. This would leave them with greater liberty and result in much less interference in the market than with present programs.

Energy

While productivity and distribution have been abiding concerns for economic policy, energy has emerged as an issue much more recently. Actually, for Friedman it is much less an issue than an illustration—an illustration of how well the free market works if allowed to run its course. "There has been an energy crisis because the government created one."[12] Friedman explains that the government did this by holding down the price of energy. Given what he has already told us about price, we can expect this to send signals and provide incentives for both consumers and producers. Since energy was cheap, consumers chose comfort instead of economy in their automobiles and a second television instead of insulation for their homes. Producers had little reason to drill for oil in expensive places, let alone develop even more expensive alternative energy supplies. One result was that supply could not keep up with demand. Another was OPEC. We regulated ourselves right into a situation where we needed OPEC's oil enough that we had to pay their price.

We can by now well imagine Friedman's solution to the

energy problem. "There is one simple way to end the energy crisis and gasoline shortages. . . . Eliminate all controls on the prices of crude oil and other petroleum products."[13] This 1970 prescription was largely enacted by the United States government, and the results were entirely predictable. Production increased somewhat. We learned to conserve. Now we find ourselves with relatively stable prices, plenty of supplies, and a divided and weakened OPEC. If we leave our energy future to the market, prices may go up somewhat, but when they reach the point where it is profitable to drill for more oil or develop other sources, producers will do so. Not only are our energy supplies safer in the hands of the market, but we also escape the heavy hand of a government bureaucracy trying to manage our energy and succeeding only in increasing government control over our lives while being outguessed at nearly every turn by market forces.

Inflation

In discussing inflation, we touch upon Milton Friedman's expertise as a technical economist, the money supply. He argues that "substantial inflation is always and everywhere a monetary phenomenon . . . ."[14] This is true regardless of the form of government or nature of the economy of a given nation. This is true regardless of oil price rises, budget deficits, unemployment, interest rates, or whatever else. These factors may help explain why governments act as they do, but the direct cause of inflation is a government decision to print too much money. "Inflation occurs when the quantity of money rises appreciably more rapidly than output, and the more rapid the rise in the quantity of money per unit of output, the greater the inflation. There is probably no other proposition in economics that is as well established as this one."[15] As is typical with Friedman, the solution is simple: print money at the same rate as output.

This leads Friedman to offer advice on a regular basis to those who decide how much money to print, the Federal

Reserve in the case of the United States. Even economically this is not so simple a matter as it seems at first. First of all, deciding just how much money there is in circulation is complicated, increasingly so in recent years with all sorts of new forms of credit and savings. This leads to discussions of the actual level of the various measures of the money supply, which boggle the mind of the average citizen. Second, it is not a simple matter to know just what is happening to output in the short run. Predictions vary and are often wrong; even reports of the recent past have to be revised later when more information comes in. Finally, the effect of monetary decisions on prices appears only months later. As Friedman's own experience indicates, all of this means that if one can get his or her mind around these various complex factors, a Nobel Prize in economics is a possibility. It also suggests to Friedman that it is best not to try to outguess the economy in the short run. Rather, he adamantly promotes a monetary policy that sets monetary growth in line with reasonable expectations for long-term economic growth and changes those monetary goals only slowly as long-term expectations change. Not only will this cure inflation, it should also moderate the business cycle only accentuated now by the Federal Reserve's well-intentioned, but often wrong, attempts to try to fine tune the economy by adjusting the money supply in the short-term.

However, the political problems of monetary policy are much more difficult than the economic ones according to Friedman. Printing money is the easy way to deal with some difficult political problems.[16] Government spending is politically popular; raising taxes to pay for it is not. A politically easier path is to print money to pay for it. Second, unemployment is politically unpopular, but government programs to deal with it cost money. Again, printing money is easier than raising taxes. Moreover, since increasing the money supply stimulates general economic growth creating jobs, it is a popular approach to unemployment in its own right. Third, high interest rates are politically unpopular.

36

Printing more money should bring them down. Since interest rates are even harder to predict short-term than money supply, Friedman thinks the Federal Reserve is foolish to try to influence them. All of these forces combine to create political pressure to print too much money leading to inflation in the long run. Someone does gain from this inflation, government. On the one hand, government gets to pay back its debts with cheaper money. On the other, inflation pushes people into higher tax brackets, increasing tax revenue. (This latter fact has faded as the income tax indexing has gone into effect.)

So why is inflation a problem for Friedman? I think that there are two primary reasons, one having to do with economic efficiency and one more directly related to liberty. Inflation confuses the signals that prices send; it creates static. People cannot figure out if prices are going up because of changes in supply or demand or if it is general inflation. As a result, they are confused about how to respond and even begin to make some economic decisions on the basis of inflation itself. Related to this confusion, some persons gain and some lose from inflation. Inflation becomes another factor about which we must be informed before we enter into a transaction, but a factor largely beyond our control and difficult to predict. Added to this element of coercion is a much more direct one. Through inflation we are taxed both directly and indirectly without agreeing to it or often without even recognizing it.

Friedman knows well that his solution to inflation comes at a price. In the short run, slow and steady monetary growth will produce slower economic growth and higher unemployment. Reducing monetary growth in stages until it reaches the non-inflationary level can help prevent too deep of a recession in the transitionary period. (For instance, he believes the Federal Reserve cut back too quickly, if erratically, between 1980 and 1982.)[17] However, he is convinced that in the long run, slower monetary growth will not only bring inflation under control, but also lead to sustainable economic growth and more employment. What Friedman really wants is a relatively automatic monetary system which simply seeks to serve the market rather than outguess and shape it. The result would be not only less inflation but also all of the other benefits of a freer market system.

Unemployment

Generally, unemployment and inflation are seen as a tradeoff; low inflation goes with high unemployment and vice versa. Friedman agrees this is true in the short run, but argues that they tend in the same direction in the long run. In part the relationship is direct. As we have seen, inflation creates static in market signals. Friedman concludes: "Both the marked slowdown during the past decade in economic productivity . . . and the general upward trend in unemployment reflect in part the increased amount of noise in market signals."[18] So inflation directly causes some unemployment by confusing the market.

More importantly inflation and unemployment are themselves caused by a third factor, the growth of government. Specifically Friedman charges: "These two aspects of the growth in government's role—the expansion of transfer payments and the growing rigidity of the price system—are the fundamental reasons why the level of unemployment has been trending up."[19] In the first instance, unemployment simply is less painful that it used to be. With unemployment insurance, other special government programs for the unemployed and the general array of income supports, workers do not feel as much pressure to return to work. This is particularly true of someone such as a former autoworker who loses a well-paying job and can only find one that pays much less.

At the same time, government in cooperation with unions holds wage rates up artificially. The most obvious example is the minimum wage law, which Friedman believes is largely to blame for teenage unemployment.[20] Less obvious examples include farm supports, trade restrictions, requirements for union wages for government financed construction, wage and hour laws, laws that favor unions, and direct government employment. He points with joy to the results of the deregulation of the airline industry which has lowered fares, encouraged new airlines, and weakened unions. He happily sums up: "It almost seems as if nobody is happy about deregulation—except the customers, the enterprisers who started new airlines and their employees, and the economists who preach free markets."[21]

In fact, Friedman does not believe that unemployment is as significant a problem in the current U.S. scene as the statistics suggest. Most of the unemployed are simply between jobs; only about a fifth are unemployed for longer than six months. Nearly half of the unemployed are teenagers or come from families where someone else is employed. Given the fact that few family breadwinners are unemployed for a long period of time, there is not a need for a government jobs program. Moreover, such government jobs tend to become permanent and, since they must be financed, replace private jobs. The solution to unemployment as with the other problems we have examined is less government and more market. Indeed, there should be no unemployment other than movement from one job to another in a pure free market. Prospective employees would have to work for whatever wage was available, and at some wage it would become profitable for prospective employers to hire them. To some this may sound cruel; to Friedman it sounds like a way for a worker to get her feet in the door of the market system and to get some money in her pocket. The alternatives are unemployment and a government handout.

Variations on the Free Market

Within the free market camp, there are at least three subgroups in debate with one another. The first of these subgroups is the supply-siders. Arthur Laffer is the guru of the supply-siders, but Ronald Reagan may be the most important believer.[22] Actually, all three groups tend to stress the supply-side in the sense that they believe greater economic incentives and investment are more important than greater equality and consumption. The difference is that the supply-siders are much more confident about the likelihood of economic growth. A recent test case was whether the massive tax cut of 1981 would produce enough economic growth to balance the budget, whether the U.S. economy could grow itself out of the deficit. Supply-siders tended to believe it could. They also feared that a too restrictive monetary policy would choke off this growth.

Traditionalists doubted growth would balance the budget and feared that too loose a monetary policy might overheat the economy producing inflation. Alan Greenspan, Chairman of the Council of Economic Advisers under Gerald Ford, and successor to Paul Volcker at the Federal Reserve under Reagan, is a good representative of this second group.[23] Most of them wanted cuts in government spending, especially domestic spending. However, they realized that it might not be realistic to hope to reduce the deficit sufficiently without some tax increases. They tended to support Paul Volcker's somewhat restrictive monetary policy at the Federal Reserve as necessary to prevent the reemergence of inflation. They talked of solid and steady economic growth in contrast to the expansive optimism of the supply-siders.

A final subgroup in the contemporary scene is the neo-conservatives. In a real sense, they are the true conservatives. Each identifiable subgroup within this diverse category is trying to conserve something. The new religious right is trying to conserve the traditional family, church, and school of small town America. The much more sophisticated neo-conservative intellectuals commonly harken back to ethnic communities, usually Jewish or Catholic, for the values worth conserving. Besides the commitment to conservation, two other generalizations are possible. First,

40

the real issue is more cultural than political. What is at stake is much more a way of life than a particular political agenda. Indeed, neo-conservatives tend to be divided into free market capitalists or New Deal liberals when ideology is pressed. Second, all share a longing for a sense of unified community at a time of increased pluralism and privatism. Those who advocate even more pluralism should pay attention to just what the neo-conservatives want to preserve—some sense of unity.

Since their critical legislative priorities lie elsewhere, the neo-conservatives have been little involved in specific discussions of economic policy. There was a continuing debate within the economic policy circles of the Reagan Administration between the supply-siders and the traditionalists, and as we have noted, there are real policy differences between them. Yet they share the basic commitment to less government and more market. Their differences flow much more from judgments about how the market functions and what is politically possible than from basic principles. Despite their differences, Milton Friedman represents them all reasonably well, especially in basic ethical principles.

Ethical Principles

Having discussed Friedman's basic theory of political and economic organization and his views on some current issues of economic policy, some observations about his basic ethical principles are in order. As we have seen, his policy analyses consistently prescribe the free market and limited government as the medicine to cure all of our economic ills. In turn, the free market and limited government are defended because they maximize voluntary exchange, which is both efficient and supportive of liberty. In fact, these are not two separate justifications. Voluntary exchange is efficient because persons who trade with one another uncoerced do so in order to get something they want. This drive of individuals to satisfy their wants leads inevitably, if they are

41

well informed and uncoerced, to more satisfaction for each partner in the transaction. In sum, the key to efficiency is also Friedman's highest ethical principle, the absence of coercion—liberty. There is only one final justification, one principle of justice—liberty.

In fact, Friedman would allow the possibility that there are higher ethical principles for individuals, but no other principle for the interrelations among individuals. As he puts it: "There are thus two sets of values that a liberal will emphasize—the values that are relevant to relations among people, which is the context in which he assigns first priority to freedom; and the values that are relevant to the individual in the exercise of his freedom, which is the realm of individual ethics and philosophy."[24] Society should have nothing to say about the latter, about what one does with her freedom. One is left free to do what one wants. The purposes served by liberty are then sheerly the personal preferences of the individual. This does not mean they are always selfish, often they are courageous or generous. It does mean that there are no grounds upon which one of us can judge the preferences of another.

We have obviously begun a discussion of the individual in Friedman's thought. At our best, individuals are autonomous choosers who intelligently pursue wants. We enter into transactions with other individuals in order to get what we want. We should be able to recognize that, in order to be free to do so, we must respect the rights of others to do likewise. In other words, we should esteem liberty. While Friedman does not believe people are merely selfish, he does assume that the vast majority of us try to better our position most of the time. Otherwise, incentives would not work, and indeed the whole free market would be less efficient.

In response to the famous phrase from John F. Kennedy's inaugural address, ("Ask not what your country can do for you—ask what you can do for your country."),[25] Friedman answered:

> The free man will ask neither what his country can do for him nor what he can do for his country. He will ask rather "What can I and my compatriots do through government to help us discharge our individual responsibilities to achieve our several goals and purposes and above all, to protect our freedom?"[26]

This expresses well his attitude toward all social groups, with the probable exception of the family. Since the individual, or the family, is the ultimate unit and its liberty paramount, social groups are to be understood as contracts into which persons have entered in order to advance their various purposes. The obvious implication is that persons should be able to terminate that contract when it no longer serves their purposes. Since consensus is hard to come by, no group should try to serve too many purposes at once. Obviously, limited government does follow directly from this, but the primary function of government does too—to protect and to maximize non-coerced transactions among individuals. We are left with a concept of community as a collection of individuals who, in the final analysis, are properly united only through their commitments to liberty.

One final implication of these understandings of individuality and community is important. For Friedman, there is no content to the idea of the "common good" or "public interest." Such notions require some sense of the interpenetration of individuals, some sense of substantive mutuality. What individuals have in common for Friedman is the desire to maximize their personally chosen wants and the recognition that they can often do that best by entering into transactions with others. The only permanent interest they share is the desire to be free to decide their own fate. This is liberty, but liberty for the sake of private wants, not a public interest. Liberty, and liberty alone, remains as the principle of justice.

Notes

1. Milton Friedman, *Capitalism and Freedom* (Chicago: University of Chicago Press, 1962), p. 12.

43

2. Milton and Rose Friedman, *Free to Choose* (New York: Harcourt Brace Jovanovich, 1979), p. xix.

3. Ibid., pp. xvi-xvii.

4. *Capitalism and Freedom*, p. 9.

5. Milton and Rose Friedman, *Tyranny of the Status Quo* (New York: Harcourt Brace Jovanovich, 1984), p. 121.

6. Ibid., p. 122.

7. Ibid., p. 118.

8. Ibid., p. 122.

9. *Capitalism and Freedom*, pp. 161-62.

10. *Free to Choose*, p. 124.

11. *Capitalism and Freedom*, p. 170.

12. *Free to Choose*, p. 209.

13. Ibid., p. 209.

14. Ibid., p. 243.

15. Ibid., p. 243.

16. Ibid., p. 252-56.

17. *Tyranny of the Status Quo*, p. 90.

18. Ibid., p. 110.

19. Ibid., p. 112.

20. *Free to Choose*, p. 227.

21. *Tyranny of the Status Quo*, p. 112.

22. The basic statement of his position is Arthur B. Laffer, "Government Exactions and Revenue Deficiencies." It is available in Bruce Bartlett and Timothy P. Roth (eds.), *The Supply-Side Solution* (Chatham, N.J.: Chatham House Publishers, 1983), pp. 120-39 or Richard H. Fink (ed.), *Supply-Side Economics: A Critical Appraisal* (Frederick, Md.: University Publications of America, 1982), pp. 185-203.

23. Greenspan's views appeared regularly in the popular business and news magazines and fairly often in the *Wall Street Journal*.

24. *Capitalism and Freedom*, p. 12.

25. Quoted in Ibid., p. 1.

26. Ibid., p. 2.

Chapter Three

Equality: Lester Thurow

With the appearance of his *Zero-Sum Society* in 1980[1] and its success, Lester Thurow emerged as the leading popular spokesman for liberal economists. When he replaced Paul Samuelson as the regular columnist providing a counter-balance to Milton Friedman in *Newsweek* in 1981, his new public status was confirmed. He soon became the media's choice as a respondent to each new feature of Reaganomics. Amid the withdrawal from Keynesian economics among policy makers, here was an energetic and articulate voice for the necessity of government intervention in the economy and for redistribution of income. Strange and new as he may sound, Thurow actually represents a contemporary version of a perennial alternative in political economy.

As with Friedman, Thurow certainly deserves attention in his own right. However, once again our interest in him is because he represents a second basic ideological perspective, and we examine his analysis in detail as a device for getting inside the complexities of a general point of view with some specificity. When we have done so, we shall want to consider other positions that share his basic principles, even if they are expressed somewhat differently.

Like Friedman, Thurow is a capitalist; he recognizes the productive power and coordinating genius of the market. At the same time, he does not believe a completely free market as described in Friedman's model either does exist or could exist without major disruptions in the way we now do business in the United States. He thinks it is unlikely that we shall undertake these disruptions. Instead, we had best come to terms both in our economic theory and in our economic policy with the reality of the moderated market system we have.

From what he has written, Friedman would agree that the present United States economy is far from a full free market. Where he and Thurow disagree is upon whether we should move toward such a free market. Moreover, in most cases where Thurow rejects free market solutions to problems, he does so because they will create greater inequities. A free market solution to energy, allowing prices to rise, was a serious problem for him because it was unfair to the poor who spent a much larger proportion of their income on energy than did the rich. Inflation was not that big of a problem because, at least from 1972–78, it seemed to have affected all groups about the same. The free market solution for inflation, restricting the money supply, is likely to bring recession, which is a major problem because it falls most heavily upon the middle and lower classes. Equality is the central value for Thurow.

The Market in Reality

Friedman's model of a free market is based on individual actors seeking to maximize their self-interest through transactions with other similarly motivated individuals. According to Thurow, one major exception to this model in the reality of the contemporary U.S. economy is large corporations—oligopolies. He contends that microeconomics, the study of how and why economic actors enter into transactions, has no adequate theory with which to explain the behavior of these large corporations.

> In sum, economics needs a theory of oliogopolistic behavior, and especially a theory of oligopolistic price determination. Some economists deny the meaningful existence of oligopolies; some glorify their usefulness; some blame them for almost everything. But no economist understands their pricing behavior.[2]

Pricing behavior is directly related to issues such as inflation, investment, and taxation. However, Thurow is equally concerned with how oligopolies seek, and often find, political protection for their activities.

Thurow singles out the labor market, about which he did much of his early research and writing,[3] as another dramatic exception to free market theory. He begins his criticism in this area with his summary of the orthodox interpretation:

> Standard free market economics is based upon four assumptions about the labor market:
> (1) Skills are exogenously acquired and then sold in a competitive auction market;
> (2) The productivity of each individual worker is known and fixed;
> (3) Each individual worker's happiness with his wages depends solely upon his own wages. Workers never look to see what others are getting; and
> (4) Total output is simply the summation of individual productivities.[4]

Thurow proceeds to reject all four of these assumptions. (1) For the vast majority of workers, skills are learned primarily on the job. High wages, then, are not usually a reward for independently acquired skills so much as for getting trained in a well-paying position. (2) The productivity of any given worker varies, is extremely hard to determine, and is very messy to reward. Indeed, if workers performed only as measured and rewarded by management, productivity

47

would decline. (3) Workers are much more concerned about their relative incomes than about their absolute ones. They continually compare their rewards to those received by other workers. (4) Teamwork is central to productivity and is learned.

For our purposes, it is essential to note that in both the case of oligopolistic behavior and the labor market, Thurow is undermining the free market assumption that the primary economic actor is an independent individual. In the case of oligopolies, he suggests that the pricing behavior of large corporations may be different from that of independent entrepreneurs. He does not pretend to know just whether or how this is the case, only that it is worthy of study. He claims much greater knowledge of the labor market. There he finds individuals who do not simply calculate their own interests, but who also compare their compensation to that of others and who work in teams with others. These individuals are not isolated. They are interrelated both competitively and cooperatively with others. This becomes the basis for the appearance of equality, and perhaps even community, alongside the value of liberty in Thurow's analysis.

The Role of Government

The world of a truly free market is an extremely insecure world, one in which businesses fail as well as succeed and people lose as well as get jobs. In a modern industrial society, losses attributed to nature in an agricultural society are now traceable to human action and thus are preventable. Government has acted to protect some from such losses through trade regulations, social security, or unemployment compensation. Once identified as the source of economic security for some, government receives calls for help from all who face losses, even those who may have earlier trumpeted the merits of free enterprise and individual initiative.

The central thesis of *The Zero-Sum Society* is that the present political system in the United States has given nearly every significant group the capacity to veto economic changes which threaten their economic security. This is an economic disaster since economic progress necessarily requires not just the expansion of high productivity areas of the economy but the contraction of low productivity areas.

> Losers naturally want to eliminate their losses, but this can only be done by stopping the economic progress that threatens to cause their losses. As each of us, individually and in groups, searches for economic security, we collectively reduce the rate of real growth and produce an ossified society that is incapable of adjusting to new circumstances.[5]

Since no one wants to be a loser and government is incapable of forcing any significant groups to accept the losses, the result is economic stagnation. In a sense the rest of *The Zero-Sum Society* is the more detailed description of how one problem after another can only be solved if someone loses and of government's incapacity to act decisively in imposing losses.

Friedman agrees with this evaluation of the political power of interest groups and of the economic consequences of that power. His solution is to assemble a comprehensive program for a return to the free market and push it through Congress. Thurow warns that none of our strongest economic competitors use this approach. Rather, the role of government in their economies is both larger and more pervasive. Sweden has its welfare state; West Germany has union representatives on its corporate boards; Japan has central investment planning; most of the competition has nationalized at least some industries. The solution lies not in a return to some golden age of free market and limited government, but rather in copying and adapting what has made others successful.

Similarly, Thurow rejects the view that our economic difficulties flow from too many government efforts to secure equality.

49

Nor have our competitors unleashed work efforts and savings by increasing income differentials. Indeed, they have done just the opposite. If you look at the earnings gap between the top and bottom ten percent of the population, the West Germans work hard with 36 percent less inequality than we, and the Japanese work even harder with 50 percent less inequality.[6]

As we shall see he not only believes that greater equality is a legitimate value in its own right, but he thinks some forms of greater equality may even make possible greater productivity.

It is enough to conclude at this point that Thurow rejects the view that we have too much government involvement in the economy. Central to his position is that government acts at the wrong times and in the wrong ways at present, but the solution is not less government. It is for government to be much more systematic and intelligent in its interventions in the economy. The results can be greater productivity and greater equality.

Productivity

By Thurow's account, the United States is falling behind. During the period following World War II, our technological advantages brought easy increases in productivity. In recent years our increases in productivity have leveled off. The clearest indication of our predicament is our incapacity to compete in world markets, especially with nations such as West Germany and Japan, in the industrial goods such as steel and autos which have been the mainstay of our economy. At the same time, the Japanese economy is growing faster than ours ever has. As already indicated, Thurow sees the solution not in attempting to return to some golden age of the free market but rather in learning from our competitors. Two crucial lessons to be learned are process innovation and directed investment.

The secret of the Japanese businesses is not *product* innovation; that is the talent of the United States. Rather, the Japanese have taken products invented elsewhere and learned to produce them more efficiently. That is *process* innovation. Central to it is the emphasis on teamwork and cooperation in learning how to produce higher quality goods more efficiently. This has implications for pay differentials, which we shall consider below. United States corporations are increasingly aware of the management implications and are scrambling to adopt, or to adapt, Japanese practices. One necessary step to world competitiveness, according to Thurow, is better management, especially in involving workers in improving the productive process.

However, Thurow is convinced that the problem ranges beyond particular enterprises. Government must get involved in subsidizing process innovation. He points to United States agriculture as an example of successful government-assisted process innovation. Through the system of land grant agricultural university research centers and the agricultural extension services, innovations have been developed and shared broadly. Few individual farmers could have afforded the investment or dared undertake the risks involved. Yet, with government help, these farmers have reached the point where their own productivity is their greatest problem. Notice that Thurow promotes the research end of United States agricultural policy, not the present subsidy end, which he considers a disaster in most cases.

What Thurow proposes as policy is a national research agency for industry. This agency would fund research not likely to be pursued otherwise, especially research which would not produce immediate returns and which addresses production processes. The findings of this research would be made available generally within the industry involved rather than becoming the possession of a particular producer. He considers this a major step toward productivity increases in the general economy like those in United States agriculture and Japanese industry.

The second lesson concerns investment. In part because of our low personal savings rates, much of our current investment comes from corporations retaining profits for

51

their own use. This compounds the general problem of investment in greater productivity. For an economy to become more productive, difficult choices must be made to invest in productive sectors of the economy, and even more difficult choices must be made to withdraw investment from less productive sectors. The latter, disinvestment, is always difficult in a mixed economy where established industries do not want to die, even if they are no longer productive. Disinvestment is even more difficult if those industries retain control over a significant portion of potential investment funds which they have generated from retained earnings.

Thurow proposes to deal with this problem through increasing incentives for personal savings and establishing directed investment. The former can be done through credit and taxation policy, which encourages savings instead of consumption. For instance, if the personal income tax were changed so that interest paid was not deductible and interest received was not taxed, individuals would probably save more. However, Thurow not only wants to increase savings, he also wants to direct its investment through either a private or public investment banking system. This system's task would be to shift investment away from the less productive industries and even away from less efficient producers within a given industry, and into more productive industries and firms.

All of our major competitors have such investment mechanisms. As a result, they have consciously targeted particular industries for development, invested in them, and eaten away (if not overcome) our former competitive advantages. The result is that we see one of our industries after another threatened by foreign competition that has been assisted by selective investment. We must respond in kind. As he puts it most directly, "Japan Incorporated must be met by U.S.A. Incorporated."[7]

However, directed investment underlines a major issue of equity which is likely to derail it politically. What happens to the people in the industry from which investment is withdrawn? Obviously, they lose their jobs! However, before that occurs, they usually contact their elected representatives. As Thurow puts it: "One of the peculiarities of our mixed economy is that we have poor to nonexistent systems for compensating individuals who legitimately lose when projects are undertaken in the general interest. The only recourse of individuals in this situation is to stop the economic progress which threatens them."[8] This would become even more the case if this disinvestment occurs by decision of a clearly identified public body such as an investment bank. This is but one dramatic example of Thurow's general theme; people's drive for economic security and the belief that government can provide it make a true market economy politically impossible. He believes directed disinvestment will be tolerated politically only if some mechanism compensates the persons harmed.

The corporate paternalism of Japan, by which, for instance, jobs are guaranteed for life, is a logical possibility. However, the European approach of subsidies and job training fits our traditions better. Whatever the mechanism, the basic point stands: "Support for failing firms should be minimized but support for individuals to help them move from sunset to sunrise industries should be generous. It should be generous for the simple reason that if it is not, we will not be able to adopt the policies that the country needs."[9] If we are fairly certain that persons will not be unduly harmed, tough decisions for the sake of economic growth are morally and politically much more possible. I suspect Thurow would support such a policy on the basis of his moral principle of equality anyway. In this case, greater equality will also make possible greater efficiency.

Taken together with such things as strengthening our educational system and generally improving our management techniques, these proposals for subsidizing process innovation and directing investment would constitute major steps toward recasting us as a world-class economy according to Thurow. But why? Realistically, nationalism

53

and envy may be major motivators. However, Thurow is more interested in the relation of economic growth to the zero-sum game. In an economy that is not growing, the total amount of gains must be balanced by an equivalent amount of losses. This is a zero-sum game. Economic changes nearly inevitably result in a change in the distribution of rewards and losses, and losers fight to keep from losing. Thus, an economy which is not growing makes economic change extremely difficult politically. On the other hand, a growing economy generates new revenues (private and public) which can be invested, or used to compensate the short-term losers, or even appropriated to the task of assisting those who have been losers for a long time. For all of these reasons, Thurow wants to increase productivity and thus minimize the zero-sum game.

Distribution

Friedman argued that everyone should be free to enter the market. If that is true, the market should be left to distribute rewards according to what people produce. Any other mechanism creates inefficiencies and limits liberty. Thurow asks the common sense question of whether this works as Friedman claims. He answers no for society as a whole but yes for a particular group—fully employed white males. For this group something like reward for effort seems to occur. Why not establish as our equity goal a society in which earnings are distributed for the whole society in about the proportions they are now for fully employed white males?[10] In fact, the top one fifth of this group receives about five times as much of total earnings as does the bottom one fifth, a differential of five to one. The same figure for society as a whole is twenty-seven to one. In other words, the earnings gap between the top fifth and bottom fifth of society at large is more than five times as much as the similar gap among fully employed white males. He calls the reduction of this differential to five to one an interim goal which can be reevaluated to see if it is equal enough once it has been met. In the meantime there is plenty to do just to come close to this goal.

Whatever this goal may be, it is not complete equality. Nor, as we shall see, is it socialism. It is just as much competitive, individualistic capitalism as is what currently goes on among fully employed white males. Friedman would label Thurow's approach equality of result rather than equality of opportunity and would reject it as contradictory to liberty. It seems to me that Thurow is making an implicit argument that while the five to one differential among white fully employed males may reflect equality of opportunity, the twenty-seven to one differential in society at large is clear evidence that real equality of opportunity has not been operating. In other words, this great an inequality of results indicates the absence of true equality of opportunity. As we shall see later, this suggests that a different definition of freedom is at work.

One further distinction is needed here. Friedman tends to talk most about how fair a free market distribution would be, while Thurow tends to examine the market distribution we actually have. Whether Thurow believes a true free market distribution among persons with real equality of opportunity would be fair is unclear. What is clear is that he does not believe that we are likely to get such a distribution anytime soon, and that in its absence we must deal with the actual distribution our present market produces, which is patently unfair. In sum, the disagreement between Friedman and Thurow over distribution is part abstract ethical principle and part concrete political judgment.

By Thurow's telling, such equality also need not be traded off against productivity. Once again he returns to a comparison with our economic rivals:

> Imagine what those who believe that all work effort is dependent upon large income differences would predict about an economy where large firms give lifetime jobs, where relative wages are completely dependent upon seniority rather than personal skills and merit, and where income differentials are 50

55

percent smaller than in the United States. Yet the Japanese have the world's largest rate of productivity growth. *Why?*[11]

The answer brings us back to the earlier discussion of the ways in which the real labor market differs from free market assumptions. The primary justification for unequal rewards for the sake of efficiency is that workers bring different capacities to the productive process and that these differences in contribution must be rewarded. If skills are not brought by individuals to the process, but rather are developed in the social setting of the workplace, and if, in any event, it is nearly impossible to determine and to reward the individual's contribution, then differential compensation plays little positive role. If, at the same time, workers are constantly comparing their rewards to those of their co-workers and cooperation is a key factor in greater productivity, then differences in pay may in fact play a very negative role. Silly notions, perhaps, but ones the Japanese seem to practice very effectively. Once again, greater equality would make possible greater efficiency.

Energy

Thurow's way of dealing with the energy issue is a good example of his general analysis of our political impotence and of his specific interest in equality. The plain truth is that when energy prices go up some group or groups will have to pay the price in less consumption of something. Similarly, while the United States has the technical capacity for energy independence, some group or groups will have to pay in one way or another for energy development. For instance, we have enough coal to supply all our needs, but it must be dug and burned at economic, environmental and health costs to someone. Electricity can be generated by nuclear power, but again a cost must be paid in utility rates, environmental strain, and potential danger. In Thurow's terms, we must make and enforce distribution decisions. This is precisely what he believes our present political system does very poorly. As a result, the response of the United States to energy shortages was incoherent.

One solution, which was advocated by Milton Friedman and dominant in recent policy, was relatively coherent. That was simply to allow energy prices to rise to the market prices. It was, according to Thurow, also fundamentally inequitable.[12] Since the poorest tenth of the population spent about a third of their income on energy, but the wealthiest tenth spent only about 5 percent of their income on energy, the pain of price increases fell more heavily upon those less well off to begin with. The poor had to get along with less heat or less of something else. To let prices go up without any other measures was to increase inequities already too large, according to Thurow. He expected the political allies of the poor to prevent this through regulations on price or supplies. This occurred only for a time. Then the free market solution largely prevailed, and increased energy prices helped lengthen the gap between the rich and the poor in the early eighties. As energy policy the free market approach worked; Thurow concludes that it has been a failure as social policy.

Inflation

Running counter to popular opinion, Thurow argues that inflation is not a significant problem.[13] Writing in 1980 about developments since 1972, Thurow concludes: "Inflation seems to have had little, if any, impact on distribution of income. This means that all wages and prices are rising by about the same amount. Inflation has helped and hurt each of us. There have been no dramatic shifts in the distribution of economic resources since the onset of inflation." Consistent with his general approach, he suggests that the best policy economically might be to just tolerate inflation.[14] *After* being adjusted for inflation, personal income went up at about the same rate during the high inflation years of 1972 to 1978 as it did during the relatively low inflation years of 1966 to 1972.

57

Moreover, the relative status of the various groups usually identified as losers (taxpayers, the elderly, blacks, women, youth, and farmers) actually remained the same or even increased during the period of high inflation. Since, Thurow's consistent definition of a problem is a condition that prevents economic growth, or creates greater inequities or both. Inflation simply does not qualify.

On the other hand, the most common medicine prescribed for inflation, tight monetary and fiscal policy, does qualify. The result of this policy will be a slowdown in the economy as even its advocates such as Friedman agree. For reasons already discussed, Thurow opposes slower economic growth. Those reasons are clear in this case because a recession brings unemployment. Moreover, this unemployment is distributed differentially. Since the last hired are usually the first fired, disadvantaged groups lose the most from a recession. Inequality increases. On Thurow's terms, this medicine is worse than the supposed illness it is intended to treat.

In the long run, this medicine does not even cure the real cause of inflation, a decline of increases in productivity. Similarly, all of the other frequently mentioned treatments for inflation—price controls, deregulations, or a balanced budget—either bring little long-term relief or create side effects worse than inflation itself. The only real solution is for productivity to rise as quickly as wages. In the long run, the only policies Thurow thinks can bring that about are those he has proposed for increasing productivity. In the meantime, the best policy for dealing with inflation may be no policy, merely ignoring it.

Unemployment

As might be expected given their ideologies, Friedman spends a lot of time on inflation and relatively little on unemployment, and Thurow little on inflation and a great deal on unemployment. Indeed, as already indicated,

Thurow's primary area of research prior to *The Zero-Sum Society* was the labor market. Thurow has written widely on the need for quality education if we are to compete in the world economy.[15] Yet he is convinced from his study of the labor market that, while education develops critical general capacities, specific job skills are typically learned after one is hired.[16] For most workers, the key to earning an income is to get a good job where they are trained to earn a good income. As a result, he rejects job training programs in favor of actual job creation as the centerpiece of his program for narrowing the gap in income between the rich and the poor. While this can be achieved in part through monetary and fiscal policy aimed at providing jobs instead of preventing inflation, for a variety of political reasons he does not think such macroeconomic policy will ever be enough. The government will have to create jobs directly.

Specifically, Thurow proposes that the United States government must guarantee jobs for everyone who wants to work. He sees no problem in finding much useful work to be done:

> Anyone with a little imagination can think of many things that could be done to make this society a better one. If the option is between idleness and work, the choice is simple. As long as any useful output is produced, a work project takes precedence over involuntary unemployment.[17]

If the goal of this program is to close the gap between the chronically unemployed and fully employed white males then the government jobs created must be comparable in pay, working conditions, and advancement opportunities to those presently held by fully employed white males. These jobs must be available to anyone willing to work, which implies that supporting programs such as on-the-job training, basic education, and day care will be necessary. Finally, since unemployment has persisted in the U.S. economy even in times of relative prosperity, this should be a permanent program, not simply an antirecessionary measure.

59

Under present conditions such a program would have to employ millions of people at considerable cost. However, Thurow assumes it would create great pressure on those in control of macroeconomic policy to improve the performance of the rest of the economy. In any event, if the projects were chosen well, the output produced would be of much greater economic value than just allowing these human resources to remain idle. At the same time, private industry would need to compete for workers by upgrading pay and working conditions, especially for those jobs which are presently least desirable. The net effect would be to close the gap between rich and poor through work. In addition to all these economic arguments, Thurow concludes that such an effort is a moral duty for a society committed to the work ethic.[18]

Variations on Liberal Capitalism

As with the free-market capitalists, one can also identify three subgroups within the liberal capitalists. There are the traditional Keynesians, well represented by Charles Schultze, who served as an economic advisor to Carter and presently resides at the Brookings Institution.[19] They tend to doubt that we face a crisis. In particular, they doubt that the United States cannot compete in international markets. Rather, they contend that good macroeconomic policy—taxation, government spending, monetary policy, the value of the dollar, and such—is the key. Concretely, they credit the economic recovery after 1982 to the Keynesian stimulation of consumption from the Reagan tax cut and military spending rather than any supply-side increase in investment. Absent the energy and food price shock that occurred in the 1970s, they see no reason why good Keynesian macroeconomic policy cannot produce solid growth in the years ahead.

A second subgroup takes its lead from the economic and social dislocations caused by the decline of industrial America. Barry Bluestone, student of plant closings, is a good example of this approach.[20] Convinced that capital is now free to move in ways that threaten workers and the communities in which they live, Bluestone and others look for ways to ease and even reverse the trend of deindustrialization. Laws that require corporations to give warning if they intend to close a factory and to make some provision for the workers are short-term solutions. In the longer run, Bluestone and others favor laws which force other nations to compete fairly and give assistance to U.S. industries to help them become competitive once again. The basic goal is to preserve as many industrial jobs as possible.

The final subgroup of the liberal capitalists agrees that Keynesians' economic policy is better than Reaganomics and that U.S. industry should be saved as much as possible, but believes that the problems run much deeper. Robert Reich is a good example of those who have come to be called the neo-liberals.[21] They are much more willing to accept the transition from heavy industry to the information economy. Reich, for instance, stresses the need to move from the rigid management necessary for large-scale mass production to the flexible organization appropriate to high technology. Often these neo-liberals see Japan as a model as well as a competitor. In particular, the United States must learn from the Japanese to emphasize cooperation among business, labor, and government, and to educate a capable and flexible work force. Although Thurow does not propose to turn as much of social services and planning over to corporations as does Reich, he probably falls more in this subgroup than in the other two.

Ethical Principles

All three of these subgroups of liberal capitalists share Lester Thurow's commitment to the ethical principle of equality.

In one policy area after another, Thurow identifies problems or rejects supposed solutions on the basis of his abiding concern for equality. While this is obvious when he

61

discusses unemployment and distribution of income, it is equally the case when he takes up productivity. While the concept of the zero-sum game stands at the center of his recent writings, that is not because he advocates it; quite the opposite is the case. Politics becomes difficult and policy aimed at equality extremely unpopular when the economy is not growing. Everyone becomes adamant about protecting what they have. Increased productivity means more to distribute, making it unnecessary to take what someone already has in order to help others who have less. Minimum incomes, guaranteed employment, assistance to workers in declining industry, subsidies for new industrial processes can all be financed from new economic growth. Increased productivity makes greater equality not just a moral imperative but also a real political possibility. Certainly, economic stagnation makes such equality very unlikely. In either case, equality remains the final value.

Often equality is posed as the opposite of liberty. In fact, these two principles share the assumption that the final unit is the individual or family. Liberty pictures this individual alone against the world; equality constantly compares this individual with others. Differences in the meaning attached to the very words freedom and equality in each case illustrate what these principles do and do not share. Advocates of liberty believe one is free as long as there are no external restraints, as long as no one is keeping me from doing something. Advocates of equality contend freedom is not so simple but rather requires resources and is shaped by experience. If I am poor and grew up in a neighborhood of high unemployment and bad schools, I am probably not so free as someone who has had the advantages of economic security and a good education. Freedom is a relative matter.

Friedman distinguishes between equality of opportunity and equality of result. He contends that the former is consistent with liberty, but the latter is not. Yet advocates of equality, certainly Thurow, would also support equality of opportunity. As with freedom, the difference rests with how opportunity is understood. Again for Friedman opportunity simply means an absence of restraints, while Thurow obviously believes real opportunity in the United States requires a job, education, health care, and so forth. Thurow may well look at results such as the differential in income between the bottom and top 20 percent. However, when he does so, it is to measure whether in fact there is real equality of opportunity. Indeed, he sets a goal of a five-to-one differential precisely because it mirrors the situation among fully employed white males, a situation most consider fair competition (i.e., equality of opportunity).

Yet, throughout his writings Thurow focuses on comparisons among individuals or groups, not upon the community as a whole.[22] Indeed, he could be accused of the crime of which contemporary liberals have been found guilty, of being captive to interest groups. He continually asks how this or that policy affects the poor, minorities, the elderly or women. Equality inevitably results in calls for the comparison among groups or individuals, and in the support of the claims of some over the claims of others. Thus, it may in fact divide rather than unite a community. In any event, equality is not the same as community. As with Friedman, the community remains a collection of groups and individuals for Thurow.

However, Thurow's concern for the comparative status of groups or individuals does open the door for a significantly greater role for government. At a number of points, government can intervene to provide greater opportunities for the disadvantaged and to distribute the rewards more fairly. Given his belief in the importance of economic growth in advancing equality and his judgment that government must be involved in fostering such growth, Thurow has additional reason to advocate a major role for government in the economy. That he is less concerned about the limits this might place on individual liberty simply illustrates further the priority of equality in his value system.

63

Notes

1. Lester C. Thurow, *The Zero-Sum Society* (New York: Basic Books, 1980).

2. Lester C. Thurow, *Dangerous Currents* (New York: Random House, 1983), pp. 99-100.

3. Lester C. Thurow, *Investment in Human Capital* (Belmont, Cal.: Wadsworth, 1970) is the best single example of this work.

4. Thurow, *The Zero-Sum Society*, pp. 55-56.

5. Ibid., p. 22.

6. Ibid., pp. 7-8.

7. Ibid., p. 192.

8. Ibid., p. 208.

9. Ibid., p. 192.

10. Ibid., pp. 200-202.

11. Ibid., p. 84.

12. Ibid., pp. 28-31.

13. Ibid., p. 54.

14. Ibid., pp. 61-74 contains this whole discussion of inflation policy options.

15. Lester C. Thurow, *The Zero-Sum Solution* (New York: Simon and Schuster, 1985), pp. 183-206.

16. Thurow, *The Zero-Sum Society*, p. 56.

17. Ibid., p. 204.

18. Ibid., pp. 203-4.

19. Charles Schultze, "Industrial Policy: A Dissent," *The Brookings Review*, Fall 1983, pp. 3-12, is a good statement of his views on an issue that separates Keynesians.

20. The best unified statement of his analysis is Barry Bluestone and Bennett Harrison, *The Deindustrialization of America* (New York: Basic Books, 1982).

21. Robert B. Reich, *The Next American Frontier* (New York: Time Books, 1983).

22. In *The Zero-Sum Solution*, Thurow does refer to community somewhat more. This is probably a result of his recent studies of Japan. Still, the emphasis is on equality among individuals and groups.

Chapter Four

Solidarity: Michael Harrington

When international socialists gather, the delegations of most other nations are led by past, present, or future heads of state. Michael Harrington often represents the United States. Never elected to public office, Harrington heads an organization which usually operates as the leftwing caucus of the Democratic party. Yet his own writings, spread over twenty-five years, constitute the most consistent and coherent democratic socialist analysis of contemporary United States society. Again, we examine him as representative of a general perspective, and we shall look at some other examples of the perspective once we are more familiar with Harrington's thinking.

While Harrington would quibble with some of the specific mechanisms proposed by Thurow, he would agree with Thurow's analysis as far as it goes. Indeed, it is a basic element of Harrington's democratic socialism to support liberal reforms as both inherently better than the present system and as transitional steps toward a new system. What Harrington adds is that the inequality which Thurow decries is a necessary feature of capitalism. Any attempt to deal seriously with inequality must finally challenge capitalism itself. He states the point thus:

> [The U.S. economy] is . . . still an unplanned, profit maximizing system . . . which requires inequality as a precondition of its existence. That inequality provides the surplus which the private decision makers then invest according to their profit priorities. Because the system is unplanned it tends to expand capacity in good times as if there were no tomorrow; because it requires maldistributed wealth to work, it periodically over-produces, not in terms of human need but within the framework of limited consumer demand which is a consequence of the organization of production.[1]

Capitalism cannot cure this problem and remain capitalism.

This is Harrington's formulation of the basic Marxist doctrine of surplus value. Since the capitalists syphon off part of the value of the product which legitimately belongs to the workers, the workers are unable to consume as much as they produce. As a result, capitalism is systematically short on consumption and long on productive capacity. Often for very good motives, liberal capitalists seek to redistribute income to those at the bottom. What these liberals do not realize is such redistribution is but temporary help which goes against the very dynamics of the system. To use Harrington's favorite term, the problem is structural; inequality is built into the very structure of capitalism.

The modern capitalist system leaves workers with too few resources for consumption by shifting those resources into the hands of the corporate elite. This corporate elite then decides how to use this capital, not on the basis of what is good for the society or the workers, but rather in terms of where they can make the highest profit. Highest profits for the few and the greatest good for the society are often not the same. Generally, capitalists over-invest in an irrational way in the production of goods consumers want to buy in boom times, a productive capacity much greater than justified by the long-term consumptive capacity of the workers. As a result, the natural state of capitalism is over-production or underconsumption. This is what we usually call at least recession if not depression.

In *Decade of Decision,* Harrington uses the U.S. steel industry to illustrate the irrationality of capitalist decisions. By his account, the U.S. steel industry failed to keep up technologically in the '50s and '60s by not installing the basic oxygen furnace as did its European and Japanese competitors. Blaming its problems on unfair foreign competition and high wages, the industry continued to raise prices through the '60s. Its primary coping mechanism was merger designed to create more competitive firms through greater size and diversification. The primary result was larger companies so far in debt to big banks that they could not afford to modernize. Having financed the takeovers, the major banks began to shift credit into Japanese industries, including steel. The response of the U.S. steel industry was to seek various other forms of corporate welfare such as government protection from steel imports.

This final result illustrates the political component of modern U.S. capitalism according to Harrington. He summarizes:

> The United States is increasingly a corporate collectivist nation. The commanding heights of the economy are dominated by multinational oligopolies with a sense of social responsibility like that of the banks which helped Japanese steelmakers destroy American jobs. The government, which is essential to the operation of the system, favors the corporations no matter who is in power. It creates trigger prices as in the case of steel, to protect an industry from the capitalist competition which the society officially exalts.[2]

Besides the trigger price mechanisms to limit foreign competition, the steel companies also sought and got tax breaks to stimulate investments in modern technology and relief from environmental regulations. Throughout, the government served the interests of the corporate elite even while that elite showed minimal concern for workers left unemployed by the industry's problems or for consumers forced to pay higher prices.

Quite the reverse of Milton Friedman, Harrington argues that our economic difficulties do not flow from the expansion of government generosity in the '60s. Rather he contends that "the basic source of the crisis of stagflation is the continuing domination of corporate priorities in American society."[3] Thus, he concludes, "The answers to the structural crisis of these times will be structural in character or else they will fail."[4] What we attempted to do in the '60s was to produce a social revolution without changing our basic institutions. As the steady economic growth of that period deteriorated in the '70s and the '80s, we turned to the right politically, meaning corporate power increased even more. Harrington is convinced that this conservative prescription will fail and that we must examine the structure of capitalism itself to find real solutions to our problems.

If corporate dominance of the economy is the structural source of our economic difficulties, then the most fundamental solution lies in changing the pattern of ownership. For Harrington, who feels he is true to Marx at this point, this does not necessarily mean government ownership. First of all, he does not oppose private ownership of personal property, including small businesses. What characterizes modern capitalism is the socialization of the production process by large-scale organizations. While the assembly line is the traditional image of the organization of a large number of people to accomplish a common goal, most modern offices or fast food chains have the same basic character. Yet while production has been organized socially, ownership and control is still in private hands. How then does he envision the socialization of ownership of these large economic enterprises? In a lot of different ways is the answer.

While Marxist theory calls for a withering away of the state, socialist practice has usually involved the nationalization of basic industries. Harrington advocates some of this as one shift in ownership. Using U.S. railroads as an example, Harrington complains that public ownership is generally only considered when private industry has failed. The government took over bankrupt eastern railroads and national passenger service when private corporations could not make money. Once the government had made the eastern freight service profitable again, it moved to sell it back to private enterprise. This was based on the misconception that public enterprise is a failure and private enterprise a success. He proposes, instead, that we nationalize some winners instead of always bailing out the losers, thereby showing that public ownership can not only meet important social needs but do so efficiently.

Harrington often refers to the Tennessee Valley Authority as an example of what is possible. Despite the problems of the TVA—its domination by corporate values, its overstimulation of energy use, its development of nuclear power, and its resistance to clean air standards to name a few—it has succeeded in locating jobs where they were needed. While this is an immense project, it shows that public ownership need not result in centralized bureaucracy. Its headquarters are in Tennessee, not in Washington, D.C. Similar efforts, with democratic controls designed to eliminate some of the problems that developed in TVA, could be used to address regional problems elsewhere. Moreover, this decentralization can be taken much further in most cases. He imagines a program of public investment in which local committees consider what a local community needs—public safety, housing, education, social services, home insulation, and so on. All of this local and regional planning would take place within national guidelines requiring broad participation. The result would be a set of priorities for various jobs the society needs done. As we shall see, the doing of this work is Harrington's main response to poverty. Relevant to our discussion at this point, a major expansion in both public planning and public ownership would result.

Since they involve ownership by government or quasi-

69

government bodies, most of what we have considered so far falls into our usual understanding of public ownership. Much of what he supports does not. Agricultural cooperatives, which he believes the national program of electrification helped generate, are public ownership. Worker ownership, such as Weirton Steel, or (in a less complete sense) Eastern Airlines, is a step toward public ownership. Furthermore, he advocates the conscious use of worker pension funds to support "socially relevant innovation," which serves the interests of the workers rather than turning control of them over to managers and trustees with corporate mentalities.[5] Finally, he proposes "the democratic and social allocation of credit" on a broader scale. By this he means steps such as requiring banks to make credit available for housing for low-income persons as a condition of participation in the federal banking system, converting failing banks to public ownership, and establishing as repositories for state funds banks that lend money for social purposes.[6]

As we shall see, there are a number of situations in which Harrington does not advocate public ownership, at least for the time being. Generally, this is based on his practical judgment of whether the particular change is politically possible or administratively feasible. Furthermore, critics must continually remember that he does not advocate public ownership of small enterprises or personal property. Yet through all of these various mechanisms, Harrington does advocate a major shift in ownership into public hands. Not only does he believe that this will lead to more socially desirable production and consumption, but he also argues that it is essential to the mere survival of the U.S. economy. This is what he means by structural changes in the capitalist system.

Productivity

In order to get at the real problems of declining productivity of the U.S. economy, Harrington argues that we must dispose of the dominant conservative explanation that locates the problem in a shortage of investment. This diagnosis is shared by true believing supply-siders such as Arthur Laffer and Ronald Reagan, more traditional conservatives such as William Simon and Alan Greenspan, and mainstream Democrats such as Daniel Moynihan. It was the guiding rationale for the huge tax cut enacted at the beginning of Ronald Reagan's presidency. Taxes for wealthy individuals and corporations were cut more than for middle and lower income taxpayers. In theory, this was to lead to greater savings because the wealthy are more likely to save more and spend less than the average person. In turn this savings was to make its way into investments in new technology which would make our industries more productive. Finally, the benefits would trickle down to the middle and lower income groups in the form of better pay, lower prices, and more jobs.

All of this is based on the assumption that the basic cause of declining productivity in the U.S. economy is a shortage of capital, a lack of investment. Harrington rejects this assumption in principle. He contends that on free market capitalist principles, a shortage of capital should not happen. If people want to consume a good to the extent that a profit can be made producing it, the desire to make a profit should attract investment. As we have already noted, Harrington believes the inherent problem of capitalism is that average consumers do not have enough money to create the demand necessary to attract investment. Absent sufficient demand, Harrington contends:

> The corporate rich and their institutions will gratefully accept reduced capital gains taxes and put the money into rare violins, not factories. . . . They will act in this manner, not because they are psychologically perverse or antisocial, but because investment in productivity is not justified in terms of that most primitive of capitalist criteria, making money. . . . It [his program of structural transformations] would do more to motivate business to invest than all of the wasteful handouts we

71

have recently legislated. The productivity problem, like every other issue before the society today, is systemic in character.[7]

The solution is not tax breaks for the rich and the corporations but income for the middle income and poor.

Once Harrington moves beyond this general issue to the more specific causes of the decline in U.S. productivity, things get significantly more complicated. Some of this decline may actually indicate improvements in the quality of life through greater environmental protection or worker safety or the broader availability of health care. A majority of the decline may have nothing to do with technology. Harrington attributes about a third of it to an unstable economy. Both consumers and investors become defensive when the economy expands and contracts so radically; neither are confident enough to make long-term commitments. Most investments likely to increase productivity take time. Harrington attributes nearly a fourth of the decline to the fact that workers are no longer moving in great numbers from farming to manufacturing. This accounted for a major source of increased productivity in the past, but, with farmers making up only 5 percent of the work force, even if they continue to leave the farm it will make much less difference in the overall picture.

Assuming that the economy is stabilized and programs are enacted which put more consumptive capacity in the hands of workers, there will be a need for investment. What assurance is there that actual investment in productivity will result? Part of the answer is that good capitalists in search of a profit would now have every reason to invest. This should be particularly the case if these good capitalists have the promise of steady economic growth and have been relieved of the fear of inflation over the long-term. That is his capitalist answer to the question. We have already seen his socialist answer. By Harrington's reading of investment, the most significant shift in recent years is that most investment is now done by institutional investors—pension funds, insurance companies, mutual funds, and so on—not by private investors. Investment has been socialized. What is left to be done in his view is for it to be democratized. Specifically, as noted earlier, he believes workers should gain control over their pension and insurance funds and direct investment of them in ways that create jobs and stimulate productivity. From Harrington's point of view, good policy should both stimulate the capitalist answer and advance the socialist one.

Harrington concludes that the problem of productivity is structural; thus, the solution to it must involve systemic change:

> So there is a productivity crisis, but it is not the one which is debated in this country and it is totally unaffected by the "solutions" which have been offered to it. Planned full employment, achieved in part by the democratic socialization of investment, would be a profound source of productivity growth. Tax subsidies for the speculation of the corporate rich are not. Moreover, the process of solving the macro-economic problem in this way would help transform the micro-equality of life for individuals. For the means would be an expansion of freedom by democratizing production from the shop floor to the boardroom. And they would also include the social redistribution of wealth which is already social in fact.[8]

The solution to productivity is not to accentuate the basic weakness of the capitalist system by shifting even more income to the rich and the corporations through tax cuts. Rather ownership should be made more public through the democratic control of investment.

Distribution

It was as a chronicler of inequality that Harrington first became well known, through his unmasking of poverty in the early sixties.[9] It remains a central concern of his.[10] Before we review his more specific analysis of poverty, we should remind ourselves that this inequality is not for him an unfortunate by-product of an otherwise basically healthy economy. Rather it lies at the very heart of the capitalist system and dooms that system to instability:

> There is a fundamental imbalance between the tendency of the American economy to expand capacity in the search for profit and the constricted ability of the people to buy that increased output. That imbalance is structural because it is a pre-condition of production under all variants of capitalism. . . . Private wealth is assigned the social function of making and financing investment decisions, which means that the possessors of private wealth must have much more money than anyone else. Inequality is thus built into the system. But that same inequality is also one of the sources of periodic breakdowns in a structure which favors, and increases, production and profits as against consumption and the satisfaction of needs.[11]

Truly solving the problem of inequality will require a fundamental change in the U.S. economy. Happily, that change in distribution inevitably will bring improvement in productivity. Just as both problems are rooted in capitalism, a move to democratic socialism will bring simultaneous solutions.

Harrington sees the poverty of the eighties as much more intransigent than the poverty of the sixties. The two factors which combine to make this true are the internationalization of the economy and the rapid development of technology. The old poor had not yet been integrated into an advancing industrial economy. The new poor are being discarded by that industrial economy because of international competition or made irrelevant by the onward rush of technology. The first reality is symbolized by unemployed steel workers. Discarded by an industry no longer able or willing to compete with foreign producers, most of these workers are faced with the choice of taking a job that does not pay enough to keep them in the middle class or undertaking education and training for which they are poorly prepared.

The second reality is symbolized by the inner-city underclass. Miseducated by underfunded schools, often products of poverty themselves, and faced with the flight of jobs to the suburbs, this underclass seems superfluous to the contemporary economy. The men have children they cannot support, the women turn to welfare as their only source of significant income, and the poor and hungry children go off to the same schools that did not educate their parents. The results are teenage unemployment rates ranging upward to 50 percent for nearly two decades in most of our cities. Men without jobs do not marry or do not stay married. In 1960, 65 percent of poor families were headed by males under sixty-five years of age and 21.2 percent were headed by a woman under sixty-five; by 1979, the percent of male heads had dropped to 42.4, and of female heads had risen to 43.7. Poverty is becoming increasingly female and young. Public assistance pays less now than in 1960 because it fell far behind inflation in the meantime. Yet, for a mother with children, it still pays more than a minimum wage job when all of the costs of work are included, and women still make about 60 percent as much as white males. As a result, women who want to work stay on welfare instead. On welfare or in a low-paying job, poor women have children who are poor, hungry, and destined to become poor adults.

The solution to this resurgence of poverty should be obvious given Harrington's basic analysis. Adequate income for those unable to work is essential. However, the answer is jobs. Essential to the creation of enough jobs to meet the need is a massive expansion of the public sector. We return to Harrington's proposal for a major program of public investment to create jobs and to meet essential public needs. His hope in the eighties is that the new nature of poverty affects a broad enough group of people to create a majority in support of his program. Harrington concludes:

> The very trends that have helped to create the new structures of misery for the poor are the ones that bewilder the famous middle of the American society, the traditional bastion of complacency. And perhaps that middle will learn one of the basic lessons . . . [I have] tried to impart: A new campaign for

social decency is not simply good and moral, but is also a necessity if we are to solve the problems that bedevil not just the poor, but almost all of us.[12]

Once again Harrington contends that rather than needing to trade equality off against economic productivity, distributing the benefits of the economy more fairly can make the economy work better.

Energy

Many of those waiting in line to get gasoline in 1979 were convinced that the energy shortage was the result of a conspiracy by the oil companies who were withholding huge supplies in order to hold up the consumers. They were not all wrong according to Harrington:

> The simple plot theories of angry motorists lining up for gas are wrong but their fundamental intuition—that corporations and the government policies they inspired are the root cause of the problem—is quite correct. And the whole process illustrates the central theme of . . . [my analysis]: that it is Washington's subordination to the priorities determined in the boardroom which, interacting with a major turn in the economy, is responsible for the crisis of the 1980s.[13]

Energy, then, is a superb example of Harrington's general view of the political power of corporations.

His history of the development of the energy problem is marked by collusion among the oil companies and their abuse of the consumers and taxpayers. By his telling of the story, oil companies carved up the oil producing world without suffering antitrust prosecution. They sought and received both price and supply regulations and tax breaks which encouraged domestic production and increased corporate profits. At the same time, the government provided indirect subsidies in the form of highway funds and financing for suburban sprawl. The net result was a wasteful energy system and exceedingly profitable and powerful energy corporations ripe for OPEC manipulation. When

OPEC struck, government turned to these same oil companies to solve the problem. Not only were these companies allowed to retain record profits generated by the OPEC prices in hopes that they would find more oil, but they were also the major benefactor of programs aimed at finding alternative energy such as synthetic fuels.

Harrington's alternative solutions are also good examples of his general approach. He favors the formation of a publicly owned oil and gas corporation which would drill on public lands. By competing in the market with the private producers, this public corporation would generate objective information about the actual costs of production. It would also serve as a training ground for management expertise free from industry influence should greater regulation or even nationalization of the oil companies become necessary later. At the same time, Harrington sees energy conservation and alternate energy supplies as prime candidates for the public investment and liberalized credit programs we have seen earlier. These programs would generate more jobs than the capital intensive oil and gas or nuclear power industries and are more suitable for the advocates of decentralized public planning. Local communities can plan and carry out an insulation program which puts the unemployed to work; they would have a hard time building a nuclear power reactor. If people are to install solar collectors on their homes, they need access to credit often not available to the less affluent.

In sum, the source of the energy problem is the capitalist system. In this case, the political power of the corporations was more significant than the dynamics of the market. The solutions all involve broader forms of public ownership and public planning. They require democratic socialism.

Inflation

Market theory suggests that when there is less demand for a product, producers will need to reduce the price in order to bring more buyers into the market. Thus, if an economy slows down, stagnates, prices should come down (or at least not go up). Yet beginning in the 1970s, prices went up even when the economy was slow. As a result a new term, "stagflation," emerged to describe the phenomena of simultaneous inflation and recession. But how do we go beyond naming this reality to explaining it? Harrington argues, as we might expect by now, that the reasons lie in corporate power. In this case, he refers primarily to economic power.

As John DeLorean can testify, starting a new automobile company is not easy. Therefore, if the established producers cooperate with one another and are not pressed by government interference, they ought to be able to limit competition. In fact they do, according to Harrington. Large corporations assume that they should make a reasonable profit and proceed to do so: "Huge companies, effectively insulated against competitive pressures by the very monopolistic structure of their industry, target profit goals and fix prices to meet them. In a recession, when demand falls, they must charge more to meet their goals."[14] Even in bad times these corporations strive to meet their profit goals by raising prices. In good times they surpass their goals by raising their prices. In either case prices go up. Corporate power produces inflation and especially stagflation as long as ownership patterns remain as they are; the most humane solution to inflation caused by corporate power is to limit the prices those corporations are allowed to charge. This is far preferable to the usual approach of slowing down the economy through monetary and fiscal policy, which results in those put out of work paying the price to ensure corporate profits. We have already seen Harrington's long-term solution to this general problem, shifting toward public ownership. If done democratically, such public ownership would eliminate profits and place worker and consumer interests at the center of decision making.

Within this broad setting, Harrington identifies four specific sectors of the economy which generate particular inflationary pressures. We have already considered his diagnosis and prescription for one of the four—energy. The other three are health care, housing, and food. The United States is the only advanced industrial country in the world without a national health care system. The resulting fee-for-service system is more expensive and less effective—in terms of ordinary public health, infant mortality, and life expectancy for instance—than the systems of other wealthy nations. Harrington's solution is a national health care system which would limit wasteful duplication of technology and services and stress less expensive preventative care over hospitalization and surgery.

In the case of housing, the problem is the high interest rates, which result from trying to control inflation with a tight monetary policy. With less money available, the price of money (interest) goes up. This pushed the cost of housing beyond the means of average potential home buyers in the late '70s and early '80s. Those who could buy paid a highly inflated price. The solution is simple enough. If inflation is controlled by means other than limiting the supply of money, interest need not go up so high.

Finally, the cost of food is kept up by a federal farm program which supports prices instead of farmers. As a result, the large farmers gain the most from the government programs and prices stay high. Instead, Harrington would assist needy family farmers directly and allow prices to fall and agribusiness and large farmers to sink or swim on their own.

In summary, for Harrington inflation is not the result of too much government spending or high wages. Inflation developed out of policies dominated by corporate interests and out of large corporations' capacity to raise prices regardless of market conditions. This was compounded by the peculiar problems of those sectors of the economy which produce necessities—food, fuel, health care, and housing, creating even greater problems for the middle-class and the poor. "At every point in the process—though in complicated and uneven fashion—corporate structural power was a major determinant of the crisis."[15] The short-term solution is to control the prices charged by those large corporations. The long-term solutions are structural and finally require changes in ownership.

Unemployment

Appropriately, we conclude our discussion of Harrington's concrete analysis and program with unemployment. For him, it is the central issue in our economy, and a full employment program must be at the center of the agenda of the political left in the United States. Both unemployment and our official target for full employment have risen in the last two decades. During the Kennedy administration, 3 percent unemployment was the official target; some conservatives argue that under present conditions we cannot go below 5 percent unemployment without overheating the economy. Harrington totally rejects one conservative explanation of this phenomena, that public assistance is too generous. Not only has the buying power of such assistance gone down during these two decades, but it has never been high enough to adequately support a family. Partially for this reason, studies have consistently found that recipients want to work.

A second explanation, that the entrance of women into the work force has forced men out of jobs, is a bit more complicated. First of all, Harrington contends that in reality women tend to take jobs men do not hold—clerks, secretaries, nurses, and such—so that only about 10 percent of the increase in unemployment can be attributed to women replacing men. Add to this the facts that the jobs women take usually pay much less, that many of these women are the sole support of their families, and that the incomes of most of the rest make it possible for their families to join the middle class, and the implication that women have corrupted the makeup of the work force becomes ludicrous.

Central to Harrington's view of unemployment is its inclusive significance. Obviously, it hurts the unemployed. However, Harrington points out that unemployment also undermines the bargaining power of fully employed workers, as many unions are learning. By reducing revenues and increasing the demand for income support, it hurts government. The particular reduction in Social Security taxes threatens Social Security benefits to the elderly. The poor, minorities, and women tend to be the first fired because they were the last hired. Third World workers lose as the United States consumes fewer of their products and demands for trade protection rise. Even environmentalists and opponents of military spending run into more opposition based on the need to protect jobs. Unemployment hurts almost everyone except perhaps corporate leaders, who can now pay less to workers and perhaps see more competitors fail.

In the near universality of the pain of unemployment lie real political possibilities, according to Harrington. It provides the pool out of which a coalition in support of a program with radical potential can be recruited. Harrington describes the program in these terms:

> The achievement of full employment, then, requires a redefinition of the institutional limits of the public and private sectors in the United States. That transformation, which is radical for this country and common place in most other capitalist societies, is a precondition of fulfilling the official goals of the nation. What is envisioned here is not, let me emphasize, the temporary, make-work, underpaid kind of job which is usually created for this purpose. Neither am I thinking of one more nationalization of enterprises ruined by private business, like the shamefaced takeover of the Penn-Central Railroad. Rather, I am saying that the public must run some profitable operations which can be used, among other things, as a major tool of full employment planning.[16]

These operations would also produce some socially necessary goods as identified through democratic planning. The

81

vast majority of Americans have very good reasons to support such a program if it is packaged and sold to the voters not as radical but rather as necessary.

Other U.S. Socialists

Socialism in the United States is famous for its fragmentation, and I am not able to bring coherence to it with a few words. Recently one major branch of U.S. socialism has been heavily influenced by E. F. Schumacher's vision of small as beautiful.[17] They emphasize local community. Martin Carnoy and Derek Shearer call this economic democracy.[18] They mix interests in solar energy, cooperative ownership, and neighborhood democracy with a very heavy dose of opposition to large corporations. The result tends to focus more on local organizing than on national policy. In a polity where conservatives have more and more control over large structures, they emphasize local islands of activism. They hope a national movement will emerge from the multiplication of these local expressions of economic democracy.

Other U.S. socialists remain convinced that a revolution will be needed. Paul Sweezy remains a central spokesman for this point of view. Sweezy and his colleagues at *Monthly Review* continue to stress the basic irrationality of the structure of industrial capitalism.[19] It is doomed economically, yet it is so entrenched politically and militarily that revolution from without is more likely to bring it down than revolution from within. Specifically, revolutions in the Third World threaten to dismantle our economic empire, leaving the United States more and more isolated. When the attempt to defend that empire leads to more Vietnams, internal revolution will become possible. Just as the means of change will likely be harsh, the subsequent economic and political system will require a much heavier hand from government in nationalizing industries and otherwise eliminating corporate control than envisioned by such as Harrington.

Harrington lies somewhere between the localists and the

hard liners. While he has stressed local and nongovernmental organizations more in his recent writings, Harrington still considers the localists mystical militants. They are hopeful sources of change who need to become more realistic about human interests and more sophisticated about social organization. On the other hand, he considers the hard liners too willing to justify violence and too cynical about democratic social change. He, himself, believes central authority is essential to a modern industrial democratic socialism, but it must allow for as much decentralization and pluralism in institutions as possible. As for human nature, class struggle is an essential feature of democratic change for him, but the struggle should be a part of a coalition that also includes a conscience constituency made up of people who are committed to solidarity not because it is in their private interest but rather because it is just. Nevertheless, all of these socialists share with Harrington the basic ethical principle of solidarity.

Ethical Principles

The basic problem in understanding the underlying ethical commitment of Harrington is to distinguish it from Thurow's while recognizing what they hold in common. *Solidarity* is the word Harrington himself usually uses to describe his most basic principle. It begins from the perspective of what persons have in common rather than what they have apart. Community is more basic than individuality. Solidarity has its roots in that basic human experience of arising from and returning to a community. It points to the reality that we are all shaped for good or ill by the communities of which we are a part. Justice occurs when we are in solidarity with other human beings, bearing burdens and sharing joys together. Injustice arises when that solidarity is broken, and we are set against one another.

The essential injustice of capitalism, then, is not that it is unequal; that is a by-product. At its core, capitalism divides the community. It sets the private interests of some against the common interest of all. The ruling class, the corporate elite in contemporary terms, puts its interest in profit ahead of the common interest of the community in human development and solidarity. One necessary result is that this elite accumulates wealth to consume or invest. Since it does this with concern for personal profit rather than the common good, its investments may be irrational from the point of view of the community. Indeed, the resulting capitalist system not only is not humane; it also simply does not work economically. Short on consumptive capacity, it is constantly tending toward recession or depression.

Seeing solidarity or community as the central ethical principle for Harrington helps us understand his program better. Surely he favors greater equality, yet the proposals for public investment and ownership move toward a much more fundamental shift than simply redistributing income. They begin to build actual institutions which assume and support community. They ask citizens to consider together what their local, regional, national, and ultimately international communities need and to proceed to supply those needs. As Harrington puts it:

> I propose, then, that every social and economic measure which is proposed in our politics be examined, not only in terms of its impact upon Gross National Product and price level but also in terms of how it hinders or facilitates the values described earlier. . . . The promotion of community would then be a criterion for the effectiveness of any national economic plan.[20]

Harrington's goal is not that people have an equal opportunity to compete against one another, but that they share a community with one another. With such solidarity would come real and lasting equality.

Harrington takes great pains to separate himself from those who use appeals to community to justify an elite dictating to the masses. It is in this light that he criticizes the

Soviet Union and others for replacing one elite with another. Harrington argues that true socialism must be democratic. He envisions a socialism marked by the protection of individual rights and enlivened by dynamic interchange between contending opinions. Indeed, he would contend that the real choice is not between individual and community. We are being driven toward an increasingly integrated community by the forces of the modern world. The question is whether that community will be planned and ruled by a corporate elite, by a bureaucratic elite, or by the people through democratic institutions. He believes democratic socialism holds out the possibility of people controlling their community.

Notes

1. Michael Harrington, *Decade of Decision* (New York: Simon and Schuster, 1980), pp. 96-97.

2. Ibid., p. 26.

3. Ibid.

4. Ibid., p. 30.

5. Ibid., pp. 138-43.

6. Ibid., pp. 143-44.

7. Ibid., pp. 136-37.

8. Ibid., p. 145.

9. Michael Harrington, *The Other America* (New York: Macmillan, 1962), was the most famous book behind the War on Poverty.

10. Michael Harrington, *The New American Poverty* (New York: Holt, Rinehart and Winston, 1984), is his most recent contribution to the literature on poverty.

11. *Decade of Decision*, p. 44.

12. *The New American Poverty*, p. 255.

13. *Decade of Decision*, p. 49.

14. Ibid., p. 69.

15. Ibid., p. 78.

16. Ibid., p. 101.

17. E. F. Schumacher, *Small Is Beautiful* (New York: Harper and Row, 1973).

18. Martin Carnoy and Derek Shearer, *Economic Democracy* (White Plains, N.Y.: M. E. Sharpe, 1980).

19. Sweezy's views appear regularly as articles or editorials in *Monthly Review*. The classic full statement of his position is Paul A. Baran and Paul M. Sweezy, *Monopoly Capital* (New York: Monthly Review Press, 1966).

20. Michael Harrington, *The Politics at God's Funeral* (New York: Holt, Rinehart and Winston, 1983), p. 217.

Chapter Five

Ethical Complexities

What we have before us are surely some gross oversimplifications—three ideological options inspired by three basic principles. Let us begin by recognizing the extent of this oversimplification, then complicate matters a bit. First of all, there obviously are not just three ideological options. There may well be as many options as there are developed opinions. What I have identified are three foci of agreement which do exist and do explain most, if not all, of the public controversy over economic policy. Yet any particular position may in fact take its place closer or further away from one of these foci. The further one is away from one focal point; the closer one comes to another. Obviously, any given position can be mixed.

Certainly, the people we have examined in some detail are not pure types at the policy level. Perhaps Friedman is, although in practice he seems to be willing to tolerate some market distortion by corporations in order to escape the government involvement which he believes will create even worse distortions. Probably because of the Japanese influence, Thurow's latest book in particular moves toward a greater appreciation of community.[1] Even before that he was considered a left-wing Keynesian, in part because of his emphasis on government job creation that wanders pretty far from market mechanisms. Harrington is often criticized by socialist purists for being too willing to support liberal capitalist programs. He considers such support political realism; his critics call it compromising the revolution. We need to remember that all three were chosen for further analysis not just because they represent different perspectives, but also because they claim a large audience.

Even in terms of principles, purity is not absolute. Milton Friedman's basic ethical principle is liberty, Lester Thurow's is equality, and Michael Harrington's is solidarity. This is true but too simple. Each attempts to incorporate the essential value of the principles of the other two.

Milton Friedman recognizes the claims of equality and community, but he interprets each in light of his fundamental commitment to liberty. Thus, Friedman advocates equal opportunity which he contrasts with equal results. By equality of opportunity he means that all individuals should be free to compete in the capitalist system. Such equality is an extension of the principle of liberty rather than being contradictory to it. He does not support efforts to compensate those who do not bring adequate resources to the competition. He specifically objects to examining results and concluding from them that those who succeeded had advantages over those who failed. So as long as we hire employees only on the basis of their qualifications, we need not ask why those with the qualifications tend to come from the middle and upper classes.

Friedman also recognizes the importance of community. The concept of "neighborhood effect" suggests a community of interest surrounding voluntary exchanges. Yet he defines it in libertarian terms as the situation where the voluntary exchange between two parties forces involuntary exchanges upon a third party. They are a problem because they limit the liberty of third parties. Friedman is very suspicious of such claims and even more so of government intervention in support of them. He prefers remedies which provide direct compensation between the parties to the original exchange and the third parties. This is consistent with his general view of community as voluntary cooperation among individuals. Thus, Friedman supports government assistance to the poor not as a right but as voluntary charity that the taxpayers have agreed to channel through government for the sake of efficiency and broad coverage in a complex society. In the final analysis, communities exist for Friedman as collections of individuals who have freely chosen to join together.

Thurow, and most liberal capitalists, would agree with Friedman on the goal of equality of opportunity. They simply believe it is much harder to achieve. For two applicants for a job to have equal opportunity, one must examine not just their present qualifications but how they came to hold them. Did they go to equal schools? Were they treated equally in those schools? Were their parents equally able to prepare them for school? The search for true equality of opportunity is nearly endless. At some point, it is more efficient to just look at results. How many women or minorities or poor persons are able to compete? But looking at results is simply a shortcut to evaluating whether true equality of opportunity is happening. Thurow puts the general point in this way:

> An individualistic ethic is acceptable if society has never violated this individualistic ethic in the past, but it is unacceptable if society has not, in fact, lived up to its individualistic ethic in the past. . . . The need to practice discrimination (positive or negative) to eliminate the effects of past discrimination is one of the unfortunate costs of past discrimination. To end discrimination is not to create "equal opportunity."[2]

In the end, liberal capitalists are committed to competition among individuals, to a form of liberty.

Perhaps this is most clear in examining Thurow's equality goal. He does not seek totally equal results. Rather, he settles for the top fifth of the income distribution receiving five times as much income as the bottom fifth. While this is considerably more equal than the present differential (27:1), it allows plenty of reward for individual effort or skill. In fact, the five-to-one difference is that which presently exists among fully employed white males. The obvious assumption is that there is something like true equality of opportunity among these individuals. Thurow is for equality, but it is equality which allows for individual initiative and gifts—for liberty.

Yet Thurow also recognizes the claim of community. This is most obvious when he discusses the need for teamwork in the productive process. The final product is decided much more by how well people work together than by the individual efforts of isolated workers. Knowing how to work together is precisely the reason the Japanese surpass Americans at this point and thus are more efficient. There is a subtle but significant movement in his latest book, *The Zero-Sum Solution*, toward an even broader recognition of the claims of community:

> America is more than a simple statistical aggregation of individuals. It is a community, a society where socially organizing to help each other leads to a more attractive society, a more equitable society, and a more efficient society than one where each individual is left to make it on his or her own. In a good society social organization is central.[3]

As this fuller recognition of the place of community is pressed, however, its primary characteristic is fairness and its final goal is efficiency. "Fair treatment is central to a well-motivated, cooperative, high-quality economic team. Equity is the essence of efficiency."[4] After all, Thurow's purpose is to put together a team which can win in the international market. He assumes competition. In sum, while Thurow takes account of both liberty and community, in the end both are interpreted primarily in light of his guiding metaphor of fair competition—of equality.

Perhaps it is a sign of the pervasiveness of individualism in American culture that no one who wants to be taken seriously in politics can dismiss the Bill of Rights. Yet, Michael Harrington would not want to do so anyway. Socialism must be democratic to be socialism, according to Harrington, and being democratic means taking seriously both individual rights and a pluralism of opinions.[5] Individual rights, then, are justified less because they leave individuals free to do what they want than because they create the sort of participatory political community which Harrington considers essential. Solidarity is neither uniformity nor unanimity for Harrington.

However, Harrington's understanding of the relation between the individual and the community is seen even better in his criticism of the capitalistic system. While his critique is structural, it is liberally sprinkled with concrete examples of individuals and groups who get hurt, especially when he analyzes poverty. What characterizes these victims of the system is their powerlessness in the face of the failures of the structure. Harrington conceives of his solutions as new structures which allow people to control social and economic forces. The powerless individual gains power, but only by joining with others in organizations which tame and channel social power toward humane ends. Whether as victim of the capitalist system or as participant in democratic socialism, the individual is necessarily a part of a community.

The matter of equality is a little less clear for two reasons. First, Harrington supports a wide range of liberal reforms as improvements over the status quo and as steps toward socialism. Thus, he often supports measures which advance equality because, while it may not be solidarity, it is better than inequality. Second, solidarity results in greater equality. If the workers own a factory cooperatively, they gain equally

91

(as they define equality) from it. There is a real sense in which solidarity includes equality but moves beyond it.

Harrington wants not just equal distribution but also democratic ownership and control. In one policy area after another, we observed him advocating policies which would produce a fairer sharing within the current basic structure of ownership and control. However, through various mechanisms of governmental and cooperative ownership and public planning, Harrington advocates not just a fairer cutting of the economic pie, but democratic social control over the composition of that pie. In sum, both individual freedom and comparative equality are viewed from the perspective of solidarity in Harrington's mind.

Why all of this confusing complexity in ethical principles? For very good reason. As we shall see, each of these principles—liberty, equality, and solidarity—speaks to the very depths of the human experience. As a result, it is impossible to advocate one without trying to take account of the other two in some sense. Each of our three figures makes this effort. This should not lead us to conclude that all three more or less agree in principle. Rather, as we have seen, the basic orientation to one of the three principles leads each of the three authors to interpret the other two principles in a manner consistent with his own basic loyalties.

If we are naive about these basic loyalties, we can easily be confused. Friedman, Thurow, and Harrington all talk of freedom, for instance. When Friedman uses the term he means the liberty of an individual to pursue wants unrestricted by obvious external coercion. When Thurow uses the term freedom, he often refers to the resources one person brings to a situation as compared to another. Is the disadvantaged person truly free? When Harrington uses the term freedom, he usually describes a person's restriction by, or power to change, the social structure. While all recognize the fundamental value of personal freedom, each understands it quite differently from the vantage point provided by his central ethical location.

The Human Experience

Douglas Sturm has provided us with a helpful framework for thinking about the ideological differences we have been considering.[6] He contends these alternatives represent basic options within at least the Western tradition. Furthermore, he argues that each of these basic options in the Western tradition articulates a particular understanding of justice rooted in a specific dimension of the human experience. We have already been using Sturm's framework in identifying liberty, equality, and solidarity as the central ethical principles of Friedman, Thurow, and Harrington. These are their understandings of justice. Sturm offers two further observations of value at this point.

The first is historical. These contemporary ideological options are in fact perennial. Each draws on a tradition as old as Western history marked by famous names, events, and movements. As related to the subject at hand, the economy, each option has emerged with a clear form at least over the past several centuries. In these times when it seems that everyone wants to be known as neo-something, we should remember that there is a long tradition behind most of these positions which is better thought through than the contemporary drive for rhetorical novelty suggests.

Milton Friedman is not just a contemporary conservative economist. As he well knows, he articulates the basic liberal principle at the heart of the bourgeois revolutions of the seventeenth and eighteenth centuries, which were an "integral part of a radical transition from a mercantilist and monarchical order to a capitalist and constitutionalist system."[7] At one and the same time, liberty cried out in protest against authority and championed the autonomy of the individual. Politically, one result was a concept of individual rights such as those embodied in the Bill of Rights. Economically, the result was the classical capitalist theory of the market as voluntary exchange among individuals.

Despite its contributions, the liberal principle of liberty

93

created some quite significant problems, especially concentrations of wealth and power. Reformers arose to challenge these concentrations in the name of equality—equality before the law at first and equality of opportunity in time. Lester Thurow stands in this long tradition. He is heavily influenced by the settlement house movement, the labor movement, and various populist movements of the turn of this century, by the New Deal, and by the civil rights, poverty, and women's movements of recent decades. All saw in equality a basic insight which should not be denied.

Finally, Harrington stands in a long line of critics and activists who believed that liberty and equality did not go far enough. Obviously, Marx stands astride that line. Yet the more radical elements in the settlement house, labor, and populist movements sought community not just equality. For instance, when Martin Luther King, Jr., founded the Southern Christian Leadership Conference, it was in the name of the search for "the beloved community." Harrington recognizes and seeks to draw upon these roots.

Sturm's second observation is more philosophical and finally more constructive. He grounds each of these understandings of justice in a basic experience of the self. There is a basic element of human experience which each understanding of justice is meant to protect and support.

We advocate liberty because we experience ourselves as agents. Whatever our sense of being hemmed in by outside forces, we act. We do things that make a difference, at least in our own lives. We decide. We pick out something to eat for supper, settle on a college to attend, choose a day-care center for our child, agree to work for the election of a congressional candidate, or leave home to escape further abuse. In all these ways and so many more, we act. To be a human being is to be an agent. Liberty is the form of justice whose purpose is to protect and support agency. It sees humans as acting, choosing beings. Its primary goal is to prevent coercion so that people are left free to choose.

We advocate equality because we experience ourselves as

94

related. As much as we may talk about the self-made person, we know that we are who we are in part because of our relationships. Parents are usually the easiest to credit or blame. Whether through emulation or rebellion, we are formed by our relationship with our mothers and fathers. Most of us can also think of aunts, teachers, friends, or children who have changed our lives through our relationship with them. To be a human being is to be related. Recognizing the power of relationships is invariably a comparative exercise. Can we really expect the daughter of a welfare recipient whose boyfriend regularly abused the girl to compete with the son of a banker whose mother read to him from age three days? Milton Friedman's self-made individual is replaced by individuals shaped in very different ways by their relationships. Equality recognizes the power of relationships and seeks to protect and support quality ones. It rebels at the thought of some receiving advantage and other severe limitations because of the accident of birth. If relationships were not so important to human fulfillment, equality would be unnecessary. Because human beings are related, justice must take the form of equality.

We advocate solidarity because we experience ourselves as communal. The agent stands alone; the related individual interacts with others. Both begin with individuals. But we are also parts of wholes. As an adolescent, I swept out the upholstering shop owned by my father. Since there was always soft furniture waiting to be recovered, the shop served as a gathering place for present and former railroad men who would swap stories and observations as my father, uncle, and brother worked. Together they constituted a community marked by an earthy realism about human nature, a populist cynicism about authority, and a sarcastic joy about living itself. Some were barely friends elsewhere and very different people on the street. The shop was a community with a life and atmosphere all its own. That community shaped me just as surely as my relationship to any particular person.

95

Chambers of commerce, supposedly the cheerleaders of individualism, recognize the need for community spirit. If the public school tax levy fails, the entire community loses. Basketball coaches urge players who may barely know (and may not particularly like) one another off the court, to play together as a team. Fraternities and sororities on many a campus try to teach the meaning of brotherhood and sisterhood to students who came from across the country and who certainly would not choose to be related to all of the members of their pledge class. Black college graduates are continually challenged not to forget their brothers and sisters whom the economy has left behind. In every case, we are recognizing the importance of community. Solidarity is the form of justice which seeks to protect and support community. It recognizes that we are not only related to other individuals but are also parts of various wholes, and the characteristics of those wholes support or undermine our humanity. Because human beings are communal, we must stand in solidarity.

Liberty, equality, and solidarity all have solid grounds for their claims as justice because each is rooted in an essential experience of the human self. Yet if agency, relatedness and community are all legitimate aspects of what it means to be human—and they are—then we must understand justice in all three ways if we are to do justice to whole human beings. Remembering our plane geometry what we have here is a triangle with one point representing liberty, a second equality, and the third solidarity. True comprehensive justice is not to be found at any of the three points, but rather somewhere in the center of the triangle where all three are held in tension with each other.

This image suggests the practical principles of balance and compensation. The analytic problem in regard to any particular political economy is to reach some judgment about the relative power of liberty, equality and solidarity in that society. Having reached some judgment about their relative strengths, the political task would be to create or preserve

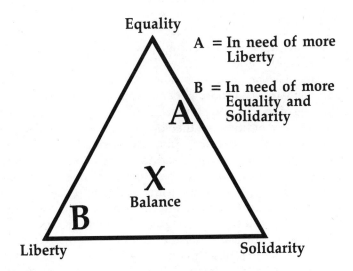

balance. If liberty, equality, and solidarity were already in good tension with one another, support for the status quo would be in order with a little adjustment here or there. This is perhaps the position of the Swedes in our contemporary world. Political liberty and economic initiative is widespread, the advanced welfare state provides equality, and history and relative ethnic purity support solidarity. In the Soviet Union, the situation is very different. Solidarity rules, even equality gives way to loyalty. In such a situation moderation is not enough. The ethically justified, if politically dangerous, stance is to be an advocate for liberty. What about the United States? The gap between the rich and the poor is greater than

97

for most industrialized nations and growing. If equality is out of style, solidarity is beyond the pale, and all serious politicians know it. Liberty dominates at the expense of equality and particularly solidarity. The ethically justified, if politically difficult, position is to press for solidarity and equality in the United States.

The immediately preceding descriptions of Sweden, the Soviet Union, and the United States are relative historical judgments. The need for balance between liberty, equality, and solidarity is a more general ethical guide based on an analysis of the generic human condition. This description of the human condition is a theological statement based on the religious experiences of gaining and losing a sense of full humanity. All three—the historical judgments, the ethical guide and the theological description—are open to debate, but on different grounds using different evidence. For instance, we could agree about the need for balance among ethical principles, yet disagree dramatically about the present historical status of American society. I find Thurow's and Harrington's descriptions of that society much more compelling than Friedman's. Thus, I am a supporter of their programs at least in their general outlines. Having said this, historical situations do change. I could well imagine myself in a different place or a different time supporting programs aimed primarily at liberty. In every case, the basic ethical warrant is to serve the fullest expression of what it means to be human, which includes agency, relatedness, and community. Finally, this basic ethical warrant is rooted in a theological understanding of human wholeness. The concrete political problem is to identify and advocate those policies which are required to do justice to all of these aspects of the human within a particular historical setting.

A Fourth Dimension

There is, however, a whole other dimension to consider. Let us assume that there is agreement with my assertion that the political economy of the United States is dominated by the principle of liberty. Sooner or later someone will, and should, ask why in a society marked by a commitment to liberty do so many people end up with the same name on the rear pocket of their blue jeans. How does liberty lead to so much conformity and such intolerance of those who are different? Why is it that when we are free to do what we want, many of us want to do the same thing?

Milton Friedman is quite right in contending that such questions indicate that we think we know better than persons making choices what they should choose, that we can have an opinion about what names (if any) should be on their pockets. Such questions arise from our desire to make substantive judgments about quality, not just procedural process. Similar questions can be asked of equality and solidarity. Is everyone having the same amount of true equality? Is shared ownership true solidarity? To raise questions about what is true liberty, true equality, or true solidarity is to inquire about substance, not just procedure. Yet the questions are there to be asked, and something within us cannot resist doing so.

For this reason, Douglas Sturm proposes a fourth tradition of political thought in the West with its own understanding of justice rooted in yet a fourth aspect of human experience.[8] Unfortunately, he calls this fourth tradition "aristocratic conservatism." Within this fourth tradition, justice is understood as wisdom, where wisdom consists in knowing what is needed for human fulfillment. If wisdom seems to be a principle of a different sort than liberty, equality, and solidarity, that is because it is. Leo Strauss, whom Sturm draws upon the most in describing the aristocratic conservative point of view, argues that political philosophy "is guided by the question of the best regime."[9] For our purposes this suggests that wisdom may consist in choosing wisely among the various basic ideological options we have been considering.

Understanding justice as wisdom is rooted in the human

99

experience of self-transcendence. From time to time, we all experience ourselves as rising above or going beyond who we used to be or usually are. We see more clearly than we usually do the manner in which our public school system stacks the deck against some children. We are able to suffer with friends through a difficult time in their life. We work in the election campaign of a candidate who holds promise of seriously addressing the pollution of the local water supply. We express ourselves better than we usually do at a public meeting, leading those present to see a problem in a new light. In each case we have the experience of seeing ourselves as somehow fuller human beings. We have transcended ourselves in some significant way. To be clear, I do not have in mind here some sort of peak experiences of pure insight. Rather, I am describing common day-to-day experiences of more or less complete humanity. Wisdom recognizes this potential for fuller humanity and seeks to protect and support it. On the surface at least, wisdom seems like a more substantive principle than the other three. Liberty, equality, and solidarity refer to the nature of the relationships between or among persons; wisdom seeks to embody a certain quality of humanity itself.

This is beginning to sound religious, and rightly so. If it is the role of wisdom to consider the best regime based on what is needed for human fulfillment, then wisdom would drive us to think about the religious core of the ideological options we have considered. Each of these ideological positions is informed by a view of justice which, in turn, is rooted in a conviction about what is most important in human life. This is what I referred to as primordial valuations in the introduction. Wisdom dictates that these primordial valuations themselves be evaluated in light of the most important characteristic of human life—self-transcendence. To do so will require both a greater clarity about the nature of self-transcendence and some considerable thought about what it means for liberty, equality, and community. That is the theological task to which we now turn.

Notes

1. Lester C. Thurow, *The Zero-Sum Solution* (New York: Simon and Schuster, 1985).

2. Lester C. Thurow, *The Zero-Sum Society* (New York: Basic Books, 1980), p. 189.

3. Thurow, *The Zero-Sum Solution*, p. 24.

4. Ibid., p. 126.

5. This is the basic thesis of Harrington's analysis of Marx in Michael Harrington, *Socialism* (New York: Saturday Review Press, 1972).

6. Douglas Sturm, "The Prism of Justice: E. Pluribus Unum?" *The Annual of the Society of Christian Ethics* (Dallas, Tex.: Society of Christian Ethics, 1981).

7. Ibid., p. 6.

8. Ibid., pp. 15-18.

9. Leo Strauss, *What Is Political Philosophy?* (New York: Free Press, 1959), p. 34.

Chapter Six

A Theology of Human Action

As one of their course requirements, many students in introductory psychology train a rat to perform certain elementary maneuvers. Since psychology remains the study of human behavior, this assignment obviously assumes that we humans are like rats in some significant ways. To the extent that this assumption is true, we humans do quite literally behave. We do the expected, what we have been patterned to do. This is not self-transcendence.

The political philosopher Hannah Arendt[1] distinguishes between *behavior* (which we have in common with the other animals) and *action* (which is distinctively human). The distinguishing characteristic of action is precisely its unpredictability, its production of novelty. Alfred North Whitehead[2] universalizes this capacity for novelty to all reality, yet he agrees that the human capacity for creativity is so much greater than that of other beings that it is qualitatively different. What both recognize is that which we are calling *self-transcendence*, the capacity to go beyond what we have been given to create something new. Because of this

103

emphasis on self-transcendence, Arendt and Whitehead not only provide a rich interpretation of what it means to be human but also serve as excellent resources for rethinking the character of liberty, equality, and community.

Self-Transcendence in Hannah Arendt's Thought

According to Arendt, the self-transcendent human condition that she calls action is marked by natality and plurality. In the case of human action, natality refers to the capacity to begin the new, so human action involves the appearance of something unexpected, something novel. While this birth of new words and deeds is the mark of humanity, it is not automatic. "This appearance, as distinguished from mere bodily existence, rests on initiative, but it is an initiative from which no human being can refrain and still be human."[3] An essential mark of self-transcendent humanity, then, is the creation of novelty.

According to Arendt, a second mark of the human condition is plurality. Natality requires plurality; the actor appears among other human beings. Our uniqueness, distinctiveness, appears in relation to others who are different from us. Like us, these others are also centers of initiative. What results is a public which we share with others, yet it is a common public world marked by difference not sameness. This public is made possible by a common world which includes not only nature, but a shared language and history as well as the physical products of work. This common world exists between actors in the public realm both connecting and separating them. It makes it possible for us to understand one another and the past and to plan for the future. However, it also provides the means to distinguish ourselves, to establish a unique perspective. Arendt leaves us with a picture of a public realm which must be constantly renewed by the appearance of the new, but which provides space for this newness to take its own peculiar place among other creative agents.

The interdependence between natality and plurality is illustrated in the various spheres of our own lives. In our internal life, genuine thought is a dialogue with ourselves in which we represent to ourselves alternative ways of thinking in their full-blown uniqueness. Out of this internal dialogue arises the new thought or the new way of taking differences into account. We call this creativity. In our interpersonal life, real friends accept us for what we are. With them we can be our unique selves, and they can be themselves. Out of this genuine plurality we gain new insight into who we and our friends are and new capacities to be something different. In politics, true democracy consists of a dialogue among different opinions. I state my position. I learn from the reaction of others just what I said as well as some other ways of looking at the matter. Perhaps we can bring our views together enough to agree. If not, I at least gain considerable perspective upon both my position and alternatives. In each of these spheres of our lives, natality and plurality require each other to produce self-transcendence.

Self-Transcendence in Whitehead

For Whitehead, self-transcendence is not just a human experience, it is a metaphysical reality.[4] All reality is a series of events, each arising out of the past and moving beyond that past into the future. To what extent each moment moves beyond the past it inherits, and to what extent this movement constitutes advance or retrogression, are the fundamental questions facing each of these momentary events. Each event forms itself out of past events on the basis of some subjective aim and, as soon as it occurs, becomes a component and a condition of the becoming of subsequent events. In this way, each event establishes certain possibilities and limitations for future events. Each event, then, has power in two

105

ways—how and what it receives from the past and how and what it gives to the future.

It would be possible to conclude from the foregoing, as some have, that we are but the intersection of influences from past events.[5] Nothing could be further from the intention of Whitehead. Rather, his basic purpose in proposing this view of reality as a series of events is to make sense of individuality amid the overwhelming evidence of relativity.[6] Action is for him self-creation; each event constitutes itself, but out of the relevant past rather than out of nothing.

The freedom of this self-creation arises from a subjective aim. The subjective aim provides the integrative principle by which an event rejects some of the past and unifies those aspects of the past which it preserves for the future. This description of the function of subjective aims establishes the basis not only of the voluntariness and purposiveness which are essential for moral action, but also the capacity for novelty which is the mark of creativity. Since the subjective aim is an aim at importance, the creative act realizes some value. Thus, the events which constitute reality are not just a series of facts devoid of value. Rather, each event embodies some sense of value; each event is value-laden. This provides a reason inherent in the nature of things for both self and mutual respect.

While many of the references in the preceding discussion have been to human experience, this description of reality as events is metaphysical, that is descriptive of everything which exists. Rocks, roses, dogs, daughters, and God are all constituted by a series of events which have in common those traits we identify with a rock, rose, dog, daughter, or God. All events, whether in the life of a rock or a daughter, are marked by the reception of past events into an integrated whole shaped by a subjective aim which then is received into subsequent events. Those generalizations which can be made about all reality are called cosmic variables by Charles Hartshorne because they are necessarily true of all reality.[7] Of course, in order to be true of all reality, these cosmic variables must be extremely general; thus, they provide very little guidance for considering specific issues, such as the appropriate political economy. Hartshorne's solution to this problem is what he calls local variables. Local variables are generalizations which are true of some specified range within the cosmic continuum—living beings, animals, humans, Americans, college professors. These local variables are consistent with the cosmic variables, but specify how these cosmic variables are embodied within those beings which comprise one part of the whole. For our inquiry here, the question is what local variables consistent with the cosmic variables already discussed characterize human experience.

According to Whitehead, self-transcendence in at least some minimal form is a given of human life. In each moment, I receive the past and in some sense move beyond it. However, the extent and quality of that moving beyond is very much at issue. What sets humans apart is, in fact, our much greater capacity for creating novelty. In this way, Whitehead takes Arendt's description of a capacity possessed only by humans, natality, and treats it as a characteristic of all reality which is greatly enhanced in humans. Like Arendt, though, Whitehead does not envision a lone individual. Rather, I arise from a past community and contribute to a future one. Furthermore, the richer that past community, the greater are my resources for creativity in the present; the more creative I am in the present, the greater richness I contribute to the future community. Again, as in Arendt, a pluralistic, diverse community and creative individuality are mutually supportive.

The descriptions of self-transcendence we have gained from Arendt and Whitehead both have principles of novelty and of harmony. They see natality or creativity as a distinguishing mark of self-transcendent humanity. At the same time, they consider a diverse community relating this novelty in its very uniqueness as equally essential to such self-transcendence.

Liberty, Equality, and Community Reformulated

Clearly, agency is central to the sort of self-transcendence we have been discussing. Novelty arises from the creative act of the individual. For both Arendt and Whitehead, this sort of self-transcendent agency does not involve simply doing what we want. We want a lot of things—good food and good sex, the respect of our peers, a carefree day at the beach. As complex animals, all of these may be necessary to us, and any of them may provide the occasion for novelty. However, we are uniquely human agents not when we do what we want, but rather when we do something creative. Nor is self-transcendent agency the act of the lone individual. For Arendt, the agent always must act within a public arena, a web of human relationships. Whitehead emphasizes that the agent does not create freedom from nothing; freedom resides in the capacity to choose among what is given and form that into something new which then shapes the future. However, for Arendt the initiative of the agent remains essential. For Whitehead, since the individual has unique capacities to seek value, society can advance only through the creative contributions of specific actors. Agency is fundamental to self-transcendence.

Community is also essential. For Arendt, agency occurs within a public space that is a community of other agents. This public must be plural; it must allow enough distance between actors for each to be a unique self. A homogeneous crowd is singular; the public is plural. Second, this public is peculiarly human. Animals need food, physical protection, and even emotional warmth. What human beings distinctively have in common is their capacity to act. Therein lies the peculiarly human form of solidarity. Community is more central in Whitehead's thought. Individuals arise from a communal past and contribute to a communal future. The good is defined in terms of the whole, the maximal harmony of the greatest diversity and intensity. Yet it is critical to

108

recognize that this is a certain form of community. Far from being dull, it stresses intensity of experience. It is marked by diversity and richness rather than conformity. This vital, changing, risky, adventuresome community sounds much like the dynamic, pluralistic public of which Arendt speaks. Such community is fundamental to self-transcendence.

For Arendt, to appear in public is to appear among equals. Our words and deeds must be judged on their own merits and not in terms of our wealth, power, or prestige. This requires that our basic needs be ensured, so that we can act freed from a concern for necessity and freed for the development of our capacity for agency. Equality, then, is not a matter of similar income, wealth or status so much as the recognition of our common human capacity to begin something new, to be creative.

We can approach equality from the perspective of either agency or community in Whitehead. If agency is the basic human capacity to contribute value, then all humans should have the opportunity to develop it. To deny such an opportunity is to deny the importance of this basic human capacity. The pervasiveness of community also validates equality. The entire concept of a social self formed and received by the wider world metaphysically grounds the self as related to past and future experiences. What we inherit from the world certainly does limit or facilitate what we can become. This is a fundamental claim of equality. But the self is also received by society. If the greatest good for society consists in harmonizing the greatest richness of experience, it follows that that harmony is greatest which incorporates as many centers of creativity as possible. In other words, the more individuals free to be creative, the greater the possible good for the society which includes those individuals. Equality among creative agents advances the common good. Such equality is fundamental to self-transcendence.

Although expressed in different language and placed within different metaphysical settings, Whitehead's and Arendt's understanding of liberty, equality, and community

109

have much more in common than in dispute with one another.[8] In each case, the mark of agency is newness—creativity or natality, and this is what liberty is to protect and support. In each case, this agency occurs within a pluralistic community which solidarity is to protect and support. In each case, this agency must be exercised broadly in order for the rich environment essential to its emergence to exist, and equality protects and supports such an extension of agency. Thus, we have reinterpreted each of these understandings of justice in light of the experiences of self arising from Whitehead's and Arendt's views of self-transcendence.

In the process, we have also responded to Sturm's designation of advocates of this fourth dimension as aristocratic conservatives. They deserve this title if they understand justice as wisdom primarily to justify preservation of the past. Surely, both Whitehead and Arendt respect the past, each in his or her own way. However, both focus their exercise of wisdom on change. In so doing, they show that self-transcendence can be a dynamic principle inspiring us to creativity and novelty. This is far from the conservative wisdom Sturm fears will sanctify the established order, justify an elite, or encourage escapism.[9] Rather, this wisdom pushes us to transcend our own views of justice and to rethink policy in that light.

The Religious Dimension

Milton Friedman's view of the world is held together by a primordial valuation. Agency makes life meaningful. That religious conviction is what finally drives both his descriptions of the world and his prescriptions for policy. And it works. It makes sense of the human behavior he observes and provides good grounds for predicting future behavior. This is precisely what religious faiths do—provide a symbolic and valuative framework within which life makes sense and has meaning. Furthermore, Friedman's faith is extremely attractive to a large number of persons and is firmly

110

imbedded in many, if not most, of our social institutions in the United States. Not only do economic institutions practice this faith, but government supports it, schools facilitate it, families respond to it, and clergy preach it. What does the United States stand for as the twentieth century draws to a close if not the freedom of individuals to decide their own affairs?

Similarly, Lester Thurow's view of the world is integrated around a primordial valuation, relatedness. Indeed, Thurow is himself aware that what separates him from those economists like Friedman is a fundamentally different understanding of the meaning and purpose of life.[10] Thurow's faith also works in providing an interpretive framework within which human action makes sense and prescriptions for policy emerge. It, too, has many followers and a whole series of supporting institutions. Much of our public life is in fact a struggle between these two faiths in one way or another. Much of the time, this conflict in faiths is described in terms which mask its true character. Religious ethics should not participate in obscuring what is really at stake here.

Precisely because Michael Harrington's faith has many fewer adherents and is much less well institutionalized, he has been even more articulate about its religious character.[11] What remains clear is that his conviction about the importance of community provides the focus for his view of how the world works and how it should be changed. Harrington spends a good amount of his time preaching this faith and trying to build institutions which will support and embody it.

The three ideologies we have examined in detail are, in fact, three faiths, each based on a fundamental vision of the value of life. I propose a fourth faith and at the same time I want to argue that it is of a different order. How can I proceed to make those claims?

The approach used by most religious ethicists to answer such questions has been to look to an established religious

111

authority for guidance. For me as a Christian, that would involve either a bit of biblical theology or the exposition of one or more Christian theologians. This is a valuable exercise for those who stand within the Christian tradition. In relation to economic policy, it has generally produced one of two results. Those who plumb the scriptural material find a fundamental commitment to community with a submerged individualism. When they apply this position to economic policy, they find themselves somewhere between left-wing capitalists and democratic socialists.[12] Those who draw upon the Augustine, Luther, and Reinhold Niebuhr strand of Christian theology emerge from its emphasis on sin with a genuine skepticism about community. When they turn to policy they emerge as moderate capitalists, praising its realism about sin while recognizing some claims by our fellow human beings.[13] Those who support a more individualistic form of capitalism have been forced either to a very selective reading of scripture or to authorities outside the Christian tradition such as Adam Smith, John Locke, or certain strands of the American tradition.[14]

In any case, each interpretation of the particular tradition of Christianity must at some point reenter the public dialogue if it is not to remain a sectarian position withdrawn from the society at large. At that point, it enters into a pluralistic dialogue in which the Christian tradition is not generally accepted as the exclusive, and in many cases even the primary, authority. The point of contact invariably centers on the question of what it means to be a full human being. By drawing upon Arendt and Whitehead as resources I have focused directly upon this question. However, by doing so I do not mean to eliminate the contribution of the Christian faith. First, both are deeply influenced by the Christian tradition, mixed to be sure with a good bit of Greece and the modern experience. Second, a good deal of work has been done to correlate Whitehead's thought in particular with the basic insights of the Christian faith.[15] For instance, for Whitehead God lures us to creative agency through attractive ideals and provides the most inclusive community from which we come and to which we contribute. In sum, I consider the self-transcendence described by Arendt and Whitehead to be consistent with the Christian faith.

Nevertheless, Arendt and Whitehead appeal for validation not to the special revelation of a recognized religious tradition, but rather to the common experience of human beings, at least in the West. What makes their insights religious is not that they appeal to a tradition recognized as religious, but rather that they address an issue which is essentially religious—the fundamental value of human life. The final authority of their description of self-transcendence is whether it speaks to our experience and hopes. Does creative agency among equals in a pluralistic community describe our best times, our sense of what is too often missing in our lives, and our hopes for what could be? We can test our answer by seeking greater clarity about what they mean by self-transcendence, by trying to be concrete about its implications, and by measuring it against our other commitments (including those of religious traditions). Yet, in the final analysis, the question is whether this is an understanding by which we want to live our lives. That is religion, and thinking about it is theology.[16]

Back to the Political World

In the last chapter, we were left with three principles of justice which were in basic conflict with one another. While each attempted to take account of the basic human experience at the root of the other two, the dominant perspective prevailed. Friedman's interpretations of equality and solidarity were controlled by liberty, Thurow's views of liberty and solidarity by equality, and Harrington's descriptions of liberty and equality by solidarity. In the end we had to choose. I argued that on that basis, we would have to reach whatever compromise was possible on the basis of a judgment about which principles of justice were most or least

113

represented in a given society. The goal, then, was to restore equilibrium among these three understandings of justice, thus protecting and supporting, to some extent, each of the three experiences of self—agency, relatedness, and community. If this compromise seemed uninspired, we have seen why as we have discussed self-transcendence. Earlier we were gritting our teeth to come to terms with reality; under the influence of self-transcendence, we have been invited into a world of adventure and creativity. How do we bring the two together?

As usual Hannah Arendt is much more concerned with making the differences clear than with bringing them together. She distinguishes between action and behavior. We are familiar with her description of action. Although she believes it is what makes us human, she also thinks it is rare. Much more common is behavior, and she takes the term quite literally. Most of the time we behave; we conform to the expectable; we begin nothing new; we behave just like other animals. We seek to satisfy those very elemental necessities for food, shelter, protection, sex, companionship, and procreation which, while shaped by our human capacities, we share with other animals.

In the Greek world, these necessities were dealt with in private in the household. In the modern world, according to Arendt, they have emerged in public and grown like cancer eating away at the public arena where action can take place. For instance, she contends that modern politics is nearly consumed by economic interests, by the concerns formerly handled in the household. All of which means that while Arendt paints an extremely attractive picture of the exercise of human capacities, she is exceedingly skeptical about the real possibilities for action in the modern world.

Typically, Whitehead views this sharp distinction Arendt has drawn between action and behavior as a continuum of more and less. Most generally, this is a continuum of more or less capacity for novelty among various forms of actuality, that is, rocks vs. roses vs. dogs vs. daughters vs. God. Most specifically, this is a continuum from an event merely repeating the past to an event realizing its full potential for novelty. Within the range of reality with which we are concerned here—humans—this is a continuum of more or less realization of the importance possible in the moments of our experience. As with Arendt's depiction of action, we have found Whitehead's portrayal of the adventure of civilization very attractive. Yet Whitehead is quite clear that this overlooks the brute realities:

> The massive habits of physical nature, its iron laws, determine the scene for the sufferings of men. Birth and death, heat and cold, hunger, separation, disease, the general impracticability of purpose, all bring their quota to imprison the souls of women and men. Our experiences do not keep step with our hopes. . . . The essence of freedom is the practicability of purpose. Mankind has chiefly suffered from the frustration of its prevalent purposes, even such as belong to the very definition of its species.[17]

These are not the words of a naive idealist!

In fact, Whitehead criticizes the usual list of freedoms—of speech, of the press, or of religious affiliation—as trivial compared to the satisfaction of these basic needs which make action possible. This is why an economic interpretation of history makes considerable sense to us. We moderns have available to us whole new technologies and social structures designed to deal with these needs—highway systems, communications networks, or the welfare state. Each is the product of past novelty, of ideas. Yet, as an established fact, they are now part of our inheritance, which is hard to change. Life is more complex, and our capacity to realize our purposes (especially acting alone) is quite limited. Yet it remains the case that the satisfaction of these basic necessities is essential to the success of a particular community and even the overall human enterprise itself.

In their most behavioristic forms, liberty, equality, and solidarity are at war. The behavioristic form of liberty

115

defends the right of each individual to do as he or she pleases. The behavioristic form of equality claims that everyone should have the same amount of everything. The behavioristic form of solidarity demands that we sacrifice our interests for the community. If we are free to do what we want, the result is inequality and broken community. Most white parents prefer to live in a white suburb and send their children to white schools. The results are unequal educational opportunities and a color line drawn right through our urban communities. The only way to establish equality seems to be to limit some people's liberty and set the community at odds with one another. School busing for racial integration may lead to greater equality of educational opportunity, but it certainly does not let all students go to the school of their parents' choice and clearly leads to community conflict (at least in the short run). Sooner or later, we must give up some of what we want and quit clamoring for our equal rights in order to consider the good of the community as a whole. For the sake of economic growth and social peace, the United States should spend more for each pupil on the education of poor children, not less, as we do now. To do so tramples on the self-interest of non-poor taxpayers and the desire of each school district, let alone each school, to have its equal piece of the school-funding pie. If liberty means doing what I want, equality means getting my share, and community means homogeneity, then they are forever at odds.

However, we have seen that each of these views of justice can be reinterpreted using the terms of self-transcendence we have drawn from Whitehead and Arendt. Then they are no longer in conflict, but rather are mutually supportive such that each needs the other. If liberty refers to my capacity to be creative, it requires other humans equally free who are able to receive and appreciate that creativity and a community which provides a place and the means for the expression of that creativity. Similarly, true pluralistic equality can occur only among people who are free to be unique, or equality becomes sameness. Such equality also requires a community where creativity can be shared. Finally, to be fully human solidarity must be built by free people working together not by smothering individuality and undermining honest interchange.

By indicating that each of these understandings of justice is rooted in an essential experience of self, Sturm implies the same basic conclusion. The fullest experience of the self ought to incorporate all four experiences—as agent, as related, as communal, and as self-transcendent—into a single unified self. I have argued that transcendent openness provides a sense of self, which helps us see the other three as complementary, not competitive. It is but a small step from there to recognize that a wise understanding of justice requires liberty, equality, and community as we have reformulated each.

At the end of the last chapter, I suggested the image of a triangle to envision the relationship between liberty, equality, and solidarity. In this chapter, we have constructed a pyramid on the base of that triangle with self-transcendence as its vertical axis. As we move up the pyramid from its behavioristic base, the corners come closer and closer together indicating a declining competition among liberty, equality and solidarity. Thus, at the apex of the pyramid (representing a maximum degree of creativity) liberty, equality, and solidarity become one. Of course, we live our lives somewhere within the pyramid, cynics say at the base and dreamers say near the apex.

An Application

What would it mean, however, if we sought to increase the element of self-transcendence in our lives and especially in our social policy? One example discussed in our analyses of Friedman, Thurow, and Harrington should help us think more concretely about how liberty, equality, and community

117

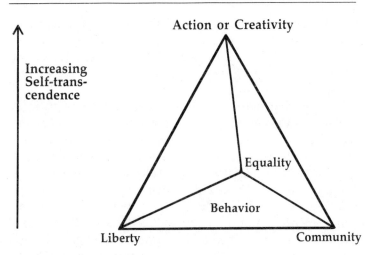

are mutually supportive when seen in the light of this fourth dimension of wisdom.

The free market capitalist solution to poverty is the negative income tax. Typically, it involves a streamlining of the administrative procedures so that the applicant need only report income level and family size. Recipients are then allowed to keep a percent (usually 50 percent) of what they earn. The primary arguments in support of this proposal are based on liberty; it leaves the recipient free to decide how to spend the money, but provides an incentive for gainful employment. Yet the exact character of any given negative income tax proposal would determine just how much it supports self-transcendence. Friedman proposes a minimum grant of about half the official poverty level. Someone with so little financial resources can hardly be said to be freed from a concern for survival to become a creative agent. An advocate of self-transcendence would argue for a higher grant. Friedman sees the negative income tax as a substitute for all other programs that support the poor. An advocate of self-transcendence would want to keep other programs such as poverty lawyers, basic adult education, day care, and job training which hold promise of encouraging creative agency.

118

The standard liberal capitalist solution to poverty has been a guaranteed income. A guaranteed income simply sets a national floor below which the income of a family shall not go; the official poverty level is usually proposed. This would produce a greater degree of income equality. Whether it would result in people seeing each other as equals is another question. Absent a sizeable shift in attitudes, recipients and non-recipients alike would likely attach a stigma of inferiority to recipient status. This is not the equality which makes possible genuine dialogue among creative agents. Such equality requires as much as possible a sense of making one's own way in the world. In our society that means working at a job if at all possible. Therefore, an advocate of self-transcendence would want to add work incentives, job training, education, and day care to such a guaranteed income proposal.

The central rallying cry of democratic socialists in the United States for years has been full employment. As we saw, Harrington proposed massive public investment for this purpose. Ronald Reagan seemed to agree, because he pushed states to institute workfare programs which would require able bodied welfare recipients to work. However, these are not the kind of jobs Harrington has in mind. Reagan proposed either low-paying private jobs or public jobs that pay little and which everyone knows have no future. Harrington wants jobs that pay the going wage for doing something society wants done, jobs with the possibility of permanence and advancement. Advocates of self-transcendence would not consider Reagan's workfare as a step toward the sort of solidarity that supports pluralistic, creative community.

For years, the battle has gone on between the negative income tax (justified by appeals to liberty), the guaranteed income (justified by appeals to equality), and guaranteed employment (justified by appeals to solidarity). Are they in fact mutually exclusive options? Not if each is seen in light of self-transcendence. A negative income tax with a minimum

119

benefit large enough to support creative agency and a guaranteed income which makes provision for work incentives are essentially the same. Either would integrate quite nicely with a guaranteed employment program such as those proposed by Thurow and Harrington for those able to work. The result would be a solution to poverty far advanced over our present system (which mixes the worst understandings of liberty, equality, and solidarity with a strong dose of social meanness). Thus, by introducing the dimension of self-transcendence to the principles of liberty, equality, and solidarity when applied to the very practical problem of poverty, we can resolve a policy debate which seems endless in the old terms.

Before this all sounds too easy, let us once again return to the actual political realities. Let us put ourselves in the place of a member of Congress who is convinced that we need greater solidarity in our society and who even understands solidarity in a wise way. Two bills have been introduced. One proposes a very adequate negative income tax, the other an extremely miserly workfare program. We must choose between legislation informed by a fairly adequate view of liberty and legislation informed by an inadequate view of solidarity. Perhaps ignorance is bliss, and all of the preceding analysis only makes choice more difficult. In any event, practical wisdom remains a necessity because the member of Congress must judge which is more important at this point—liberty which is informed by self-transcendence or solidarity which is not. Add to this the calculation of the relative possibilities of passage, veto, and effective administration, and we are once more brought back to the critical importance of practical political judgment. Moreover, we have complicated matters in some ways for practical wisdom by placing the choice within a pyramid rather than a relatively simple triangle.

Such is often the role of successful social ethics. It identifies alternative courses of action with particular attention to the value dimension of each. It considers those value dimensions

120

in light of insights into the value of human life itself. It then returns to the policy debate, but often with new complexity born of new insight. Perhaps the simplest policy is one which ignores these matters of value. Is it the most humane? Our inquiry in this chapter suggests not. Let us proceed, then, to ask some further questions about our current public debate over economic policy in light of the insights we have gained so far.

Notes

1. Hannah Arendt, *The Human Condition* (Garden City, N.Y.: Doubleday, 1959), is the best source for her basic discussion of the human action. *On Revolution* (New York: Viking Press, 1956) relates her thought to economics and to equality and solidarity in particular.

2. Alfred North Whitehead, *The Adventure of Ideas* (New York: Free Press, 1967), is the best single source of his thinking on the human action. *Process and Reality* (New York: Free Press, 1969) is the standard source on his general metaphysics.

3. Hannah Arendt, *The Human Condition*, p. 176.

4. Lois Gehr Livezey and Douglas Sturm have done those of us influenced by Whitehead's thought and also committed to justice a great service by seeking much greater specificity about the implications of the former for the latter. See Lois Gehr Livezey, "Rights, Goods, and Virtues: Toward an Interpretation of Justice in Process Thought," *The Annual of the Society of Christian Ethics: 1986* (Knoxville, Tenn.: Society of Christian Ethics, 1986), pp. 37-64, and Douglas Sturm, "Process Thought and Political Theory: Implications of a Principle of Internal Relations" in John B. Cobb, Jr., and W. Widick Schroeder, *Process Philosophy and Social Thought* (Chicago: Center for the Scientific Study of Religion, 1981), pp. 81-102.

5. See, for instance, Max L. Stackhouse, "The Perils of Process: A Response to Sturm," and Henry W. Clark,

"Process Thought and Justice," both in Cobb and Schroeder, *Process Philosophy and Social Thought*, pp. 103-12 and 132-40, respectively, for some of the implications drawn from this evaluation of process thought.

6. An example of this tendency to stress community and relationship at the expense of individuality is Bernard M. Loomer, "Theology in the American Grain," in Cobb and Schroeder, *Process Philosophy and Social Thought*, pp. 141-52. Livezey, "Goods, Rights and Virtues," and Sturm, "Process Thought and Political Theory," seek to address this problem.

7. Charles Hartshorne, "The Cosmic Variables," in *Beyond Humanism* (Lincoln: University of Nebraska Press, 1968), pp. 110-24.

8. Indeed, I would argue that Whitehead's metaphysics provides a coherent context for Arendt's account of the human condition. However, that would take more space than is justified here. The argument would take much the same form as that Franklin I. Gamwell uses to place John Dewey within a Whiteheadian framework in Franklin I. Gamwell, *Beyond Preference* (Chicago: University of Chicago Press, 1984).

9. Douglas Sturm, "The Prism of Justice," *The Annual of the Society of Christian Ethics: 1981* (Dallas, Tex.: Society of Christian Ethics, 1981), p. 66.

10. Lester Thurow, "Why Do Economists Disagree?" *Dissent* 29 (Spring 1982): 176-82.

11. Michael Harrington, *The Politics at God's Funeral* (New York: Holt, Rinehart and Winston, 1983).

12. As we shall see, this was the approach of the Catholic bishops in their pastoral letter on the United States economy. See National Conference of Catholic Bishops, *Economic Justice for All* (Washington: United States Catholic Conference, 1986). Other good examples are J. Philip Wogaman, *Economics and Ethics* (Philadelphia: Fortress Press, 1986) and Prentiss L. Pemberton and Daniel Rush Finn, *Toward a Christian Economic Ethic* (Minneapolis: Winston Press, 1985).

13. Robert Benne, *The Ethic of Democratic Capitalism* (Philadelphia: Fortress Press, 1981), is the best example.

14. Michael Novak is a good example of this approach. See Michael Novak, *The Spirit of Democratic Capitalism* (New York: Simon and Schuster, 1982), or the document he influenced greatly, Lay Commission on Catholic Social Teaching and the U.S. Economy, *Toward the Future* (New York: Lay Commission on Catholic Social Teaching and the U.S. Economy, 1984).

15. Two good introductions to this task are John B. Cobb, Jr., and David Ray Griffin, *Process Theology: An Introductory Exposition* (Philadelphia: Westminster Press, 1976), and Delwin Brown, Ralph E. James, Jr., and Gene Reeves (eds.), *Process Philosophy and Christian Thought* (Indianapolis: Bobbs-Merrill, 1971) especially Bernard M. Loomer, "Christian Faith and Process Philosophy," pp. 70-98.

16. Alan Anderson and George Pickering develop a similar analysis of religion in relation to racism in the United States in Alan B. Anderson and George W. Pickering, *Confronting the Color Line* (Athens, Ga.: University of Georgia Press, 1986), especially pages 389-410.

17. Whitehead, *Adventure of Ideas*, p. 66.

Chapter Seven

Economic Justice for All

Social activists within the mainline Protestant denomina-
tions in the United States cannot help envying the drafters of
the pastoral letter of the National Conference of Catholic
Bishops, *Economic Justice for All*.[1] First of all, we write and our
official bodies adopt statements and study documents by the
hundreds each year without *Newsweek* and *Time*—let alone
CBS, NBC, and ABC—ever noticing. We have probably done
it too long and too often. The National Conference of Bishops
has shown great media sense in limiting their attention to
nuclear war in 1983 and the economy in 1986. They also
displayed considerable political and institutional wisdom.
There may even be time for these Pastoral Letters to sink in
both inside and outside the Catholic Church before others
come along.

However, the media interest arises from more than the
infrequency of social statements from the bishops. There is
the implication carried within the very term "pastoral letter"
that this document is intended to filter through the
institutional structure of the Catholic Church in the United

States in a much more systematic fashion than is generally the case with comparable Protestant documents. In addition, there is much more institutional structure through which to filter, an extensive parochial school system in particular. Finally, the bishops retain much more of an aura of authority than do most Protestant church leaders. Catholics may find this last point laughable when they compare the pluralism of the contemporary church with the past. Surely this claim to authority will be tested when, or if, a Catholic member of the local Chamber of Commerce reads the letter. Regardless, by comparison with religious leaders of the moderate to liberal Protestant groups, the bishops are attributed more authority and can marshall greater institutional resources when they issue such a social statement.

All of these matters are worthy of further study. How they intersect with the present political climate and the institutional problems of the contemporary Catholic Church in the United States should also be investigated. These practical political and institutional concerns may even go a long way toward explaining much of the content of the pastoral. However, we shall consider here how the document does what it claims to do, to relate the Catholic moral tradition to the economy of the United States. To do so is not to ignore these other considerations. We may even have better grounds for thinking about them when we are through, as we shall see.

In the terms we developed in the last chapter, I propose to take up *Economic Justice for All* as an attempt by the bishops to bring wisdom to bear upon the contemporary debate among ideological options in the United States. That wisdom is drawn from both a reading of the present times and the Catholic moral tradition. Embodied within that wisdom is a view or views of human nature, of what is needed for full human development. Issuing forth from this wisdom is both a general perspective on what sort of regime is appropriate to the present social, political, and economic context in the United States and specific policy proposals designed to

126

advance such a regime. The central question before us is whether this wisdom is up to the task at hand.

The Moral Position of the Pastoral

After a brief description of the human importance of economic arrangements, the central problems facing the present U.S. economy, and the need for moral vision, the bishops turn to "The Christian Vision of Economic Life" with these words:

> The basis for all that the Church believes about the moral dimensions of economic life is its vision of the transcendent worth—the sacredness—of human beings. *The dignity of the human person, realized in community with others, is the criterion against which all aspects of economic life must be measured.* All human beings, therefore, are ends to be served by the institutions which make up the economy, not means to be exploited for more narrowly defined goals. Human person-hood must be respected with a reverence that is religious. (par. 28)

Two somewhat contrary conclusions can be drawn from this summary statement. First, the bishops are assuming the stance of wisdom as described by Leo Strauss. They claim insight into what is best for human beings. In some senses, this leads them to stand above the usual ideological conflict, which may help explain why the popular media has had difficulty pigeonholing their position. At the same time, the bishops' principles emphasize community as essential to human fulfillment from the beginning. This centrality of community in their most abstract formulation has implications both for more proximate ethical standards and for policy judgments, as we shall see.

When the bishops turn to the Hebrew Scriptures, the centrality of community is confirmed. The creation account affirms both that the created world is good and that every person possesses the dignity attached to being created in the image of God. The Fall is interpreted as introducing

127

alienation not just from God but also from other humans. It "shatters the solidarity of the human community" (par. 33). It is not unimportant that sin is discussed quickly here and then plays such a minor role in the rest of their analysis. This is in stark contrast to most justifications of capitalism by Christian ethicists, which base much of their case on the power of sin. The bishops move on very quickly to an extended discussion of covenant that stresses how the covenant with God provided the foundation for a just community. The bishops summarize the message of the Hebrew Scriptures in very communitarian terms:

> Every human person is created as an image of God, and the denial of dignity to a person is a blot on this image. Creation is a gift to all men and women, not to be appropriated for the benefit of a few; its beauty is an object of joy and reverence. The same God who came to the aid of an oppressed people and formed them into a covenant community continues to hear the cries of the oppressed and to create communities which are responsive to God's word. God's love and life are present when people can live in a community of faith and hope. (par. 40)

When the bishops turn to the New Testament, the emphasis remains the same. The new covenant establishes a new community of love and mutual support. To become a disciple is to join with others in the love of God and of neighbor, even if that involves sacrifice. Drawing heavily upon the Gospel of Luke, the bishops stress the unique status of the poor, as objects of God's special love and the Christian community's particular concern while noting the dangers of great wealth. From this they draw support for the "preferential option for the poor" which we shall consider below. This survey of the scriptures ends with a note of hope:

> Christian communities that commit themselves to solidarity with those suffering and to confrontation with those attitudes and ways of acting which institutionalize injustice, will themselves experience the power and presence of Christ. They will embody in their lives the values of the new creation while

they labor under the old. The quest for economic and social justice will always combine hope and realism . . . (par. 55)

As read by the bishops, the core of the biblical tradition is communitarian from beginning to end. This is but the beginning.

The bishops shift from Scripture to tradition by means of reference to natural law. They affirm the natural law tradition in arguing that the ethical perspective they are to lay out is intelligible to all humans whether Christian or not because "human understanding and religious belief are complimentary, not contradictory" (par. 61). The communitarian core of this ethical perspective is crystal clear from the very beginning: "Human life is life in community. Catholic social teaching proposes several complementary perspectives that show how moral responsibilities and duties in the economic sphere are rooted in this call to community" (par. 63). The bishops proceed to develop the inherently social character of human life, and this implies both dependence on and responsibility to the commonwealth. They conclude: "Solidarity is another name for this social friendship and civic commitment that make human moral and economic life possible" (par. 66).

What follows is an interpretation of the traditional categories of commutative, social, and distributive justice in terms of participation in community. Negatively, the central problem for justice is marginalization—whether political, economic, or social.

> Stated positively, justice demands that social institutions be ordered in a way that guarantees all persons the ability to participate actively in the economic, political, and cultural life of society. . . . Such participation is an essential expression of the social nature of human beings and of their communitarian vocation. (par. 77)

Human rights receive comparable treatment. They are first given a communitarian interpretation in principle: "The biblical emphasis on covenant and community . . . show[s]

129

that human dignity can only be realized and protected in solidarity with others" (par. 79). They are also broadened to include economic rights such as the basic necessities, employment, and property ownership. The final rationale is familiar: "These fundamental rights . . . state the minimum conditions for economic institutions that respect human dignity, social solidarity, and justice. . . . Any denial of these rights harms persons and wounds the human community" (par. 80). Throughout the discussion of justice and human rights, the fundamental moral principle which shapes and justifies these more proximate principles is human solidarity.

When the bishops turn to the theme which has drawn the most attention, the "preferential option for the poor," this moral context remains crucial. The argument here runs that the common good requires justice for all, which in turn implies particular support for those who are most the victims of injustice. Therefore, "Those who are marginalized and whose rights are denied have privileged claims if society is to provide justice for *all*" (par. 87). If the option for the poor is rooted in the common good, it is based in community. The bishops do not leave this conclusion unstated:

> The prime purpose of this special commitment to the poor is to enable them to become active participants in the life of society. It is to enable *all* persons to share in and contribute to the common good. The "option for the poor," therefore, is not an adversarial slogan which pits one group or class against another. Rather it states that the deprivation and powerlessness of the poor wounds the whole community. The extent of their suffering is a measure of how far we are from being a true community of persons. (par. 88)

On this basis, the bishops propose three priorities for social policy—meeting the basic needs of the poor, increasing the participation of the marginalized, and directing investment to benefit the poor. Commentators have emphasized this commitment to equality without tracing its roots back into community.

This chapter concludes with a section outlining the rights and responsibilities of workers, owners and managers, and citizens. Workers have the right to work, to a just wage, and to organize. In return, workers have the responsibilities to work hard and well and to show concern for the disadvantaged both directly and through their labor organizations. The Catholic tradition defends the right of private ownership to stimulate creativity and disperse power. However, this does not justify unlimited accumulation of wealth and must be tempered by a sense of stewardship which recognizes that everything is finally a gift from God. Citizens have the responsibility to assist one another simply because they are members of the same society. Since this shared social life is broader and richer than government can or should include, Catholic teachings have placed limits on control by the central government. However, they have consistently recognized a positive role for government in protecting human rights and securing justice. The principle of subsidiarity attempts to address this positive but limited function of government by stating that "government should undertake only those initiatives which exceed the capacity of individuals or private groups acting independently" (par. 124). In all three cases—workers, owners and managers, and citizens—the final criteria for balancing rights and responsibilities is the common good, the needs of the community.

I have belabored this section on "The Christian Vision of Economic Life" and quoted from it extensively for good reasons. It has been largely ignored by the popular media. It, not the policy recommendations, constitutes the uniquely Catholic contribution of the document. Once we recognize the centrality of community, this discussion holds together in a more coherent way than may at first appear. It is, as we shall see, not entirely consistent with the policy recommendations which follow. Finally, its thorough advocacy of solidarity and community, especially when contrasted with its policy recommendations and with other descriptions of

131

solidarity, raises some very basic issues about the meaning of this central principle.

The Policy Recommendations of the Pastoral

While greater in number and quite complex, the policy recommendations of the bishops can be summarized much more quickly for our purposes. The bishops begin their policy discussion by stating once again that they are taking the position we have identified with wisdom:

> In short, the church is not bound to any particular economic, political, or social system; it has lived with many forms of economic and social organization, and will continue to do so evaluating each according to moral and ethical principles: What is the impact of the system on people? Does it support or threaten the realization of human dignity. (par. 130)

On this basis, they proceed to reject both free market capitalism and radical socialism, refuse to propose a third way, and endorse reforming the present system. We shall return to this discussion later. They then identify four economic policy issues they want to address in detail—unemployment, poverty, food and agriculture, and international economy concerns. In what follows they lay out the problem, suggest the basic moral concern in relation to it, and propose specific policy in each case.

The bishops see full employment as the first priority for domestic economic policy. This is justified morally by a familiar communitarian principle, the right to participate: "Employment is a basic right, a right which protects the freedom of all to participate in the economic life of society. It is a right which flows from the principles of justice which we have outlined above" (par. 137). The bishops then survey both the scope and composition of unemployment and its newer forms fueled by technological change and foreign competition. When they turn to policy, the bishops do sound like the familiar liberals described by the popular media.

132

While endorsing the coordination of fiscal and monetary policy to reduce unemployment, deficit reduction and tax policies that encourage investment, they are adamant that full employment not be sacrificed to control inflation. Beyond these general policies, they advocate job training and job creation. While always balancing private and public jobs, they do come down behind a public employment program aimed at meeting "society's social needs that are going unmet" (par. 165).

After laying out the data on poverty and distribution of income and wealth, the bishops turn to principles and thus to participation in community. While allowing that Catholic social teaching does not require total equality, the bishops conclude:

> These norms establish a strong presumption against extreme inequality of income and wealth as long as there are poor, hungry, and homeless people in our midst. They also suggest that extreme inequalities are detrimental to the development of social solidarity and community. In view of these norms we find the disparities of income and wealth in the United States to be unacceptable. (par. 185)

In shifting to policy recommendation, the tone turns nearly radical. "The principle of social solidarity suggests that alleviating poverty will require fundamental changes in social and economic structures" (par. 187). What constitutes fundamental change is always debatable, but what follows seems hardly radical. Since work includes one in the economic mainstream, it is their preferred policy solution, as we have seen. Beyond this, antidiscrimination, tax reform, support for education and day care, and welfare reform compose a very standard liberal prescription. It sounds much like the platform of the Democratic party.

The section on Food and Agriculture is essentially a defense of the family farm. The values of the way of life of the small and medium size farmer are celebrated as well as the economic efficiency of competition among many relatively

133

small producers. Recommended policies include immediate assistance with farm debts and the more long-term targeting of Federal support programs and research to support the family farm. Perhaps because the section was added late in the drafting process, it does not integrate into the overall moral argument very well. Its policies do fit in quite well with the liberal capitalist line we have been noting.

Finally, the bishops address the world economy. In their view, the key issue in the international economy is relations between the rich north and the poor south. Their description follows the general outline of a dependency analysis, according to which the poor nations are subordinated by the wealthy often through the actions of transnational corporations. On similar bases, many liberation theologians call for a revolution in their society and in the international economic system. The U.S. bishops propose reform:

> These perspectives constitute a call for fundamental reform in the international economic order. . . . We urge, as a basic and overriding consideration, that both empirical and moral evidence . . . calls for the revival of the dialogue between the industrialized countries of the North and the developing countries of the South, with the aim of reorganizing international economic relations to establish greater equality and help meet the basic human needs of the poor majority. (par. 259)

This fundamental reform ought to sound familiar to liberal internationalists. It involves providing larger amounts of development assistance to meet basic needs through multilateral agencies, reducing trade restrictions on poor nations, easing the debt of poor nations, developing a code of conduct for foreign private investment, and increased food aid linked to assistance to Third World farmers (pars. 261-87).

One final set of recommendations has been set off by themselves for the sake of emphasis. Here the terms are cooperation and partnership not solidarity and community. Within industries and firms, cooperation mostly means less conflict between labor and management based both on a more participatory approach to management and more flexibility on the part of unions. On the local and regional level, cooperation comes down mostly to community development corporations and enterprise zones. At the national level, cooperation involves government and private groups planning together. However, the bishops are quick to note the negative reaction to government planning in the United States and to make clear they have in mind not a highly centralized role for government, but one which will "work *in partnership with* the many other groups in society, helping them fulfill their tasks and responsibilities more effectively, not replacing or destroying them" (par. 314). On the international level, cooperation refers to voluntarily joining in the efforts of the international institutions already discussed in the earlier section on that topic. Throughout, the emphasis is on the voluntary participation of individuals and groups in cooperative efforts to meet human needs. What liberal could disagree?

The Gap Between Principles and Policies

We can fairly summarize what we have found by saying that in the commonly accepted terms of Western political philosophy the bishops have developed a socialist rationale for liberal capitalist policy recommendations. In principle, they argue long and hard for solidarity and community. In practice, they advocate reforms designed primarily to bring greater equality within a basically capitalist system. It is a sad commentary on the nature of contemporary public discussion that the bishops were identified and criticized for being leftists on the basis of their support for liberal policy with little recognition of their apparently more radical principles.

How do we understand this dissonance between principles and policy, and just how radical are the bishops' principles anyway? One possible explanation for the apparent inconsistencies is politics among the bishops. After all, this is the product of a committee and had to be approved

135

by an assembly of bishops with very different political stances. This does not explain why the rationale appears to be to the left of the policy recommendations. Conservatives are not noticeably less interested in theory than in practice. If compromises had to be made, why not make them at both levels? Another political explanation has to do with the broader political climate. Some have described the Reagan appeal in terms of an outbreak of selfishness in American society. The pastoral letter, then, could be seen as a response to Reagan that took up the challenge at both the level of principle, where he, too, was more radical, and at the level of policy where both the President and the bishops were forced to be more pragmatic. If this is true, why did the bishops wait until after the 1984 election to endorse Mondale's position? Or did they recognize that his cause was lost and prefer not to bear the cross with him? Finally, some see this and the former pastoral on peace as an attempt to show that the Catholic Church cares about life after birth as well as before, in order to disarm critics of the Church's lobbying efforts on abortion. If so, this represents an immense investment of time and effort when simpler means are available through the Washington offices of the Church. All of these political explanations are probably partially correct. None convincingly justifies the apparently radical character of the ethical materials or the gap between them and policy.

Perhaps the explanation exists at a deeper level with more abiding significance. Are not moral principles, and especially religious resources, more eternal than social policy? As such, are they not both more permanent and more pure? One variant on this theme, typically more prominent in Protestant circles, is that although religious ideals may speak of love and solidarity, social policy must take account of human sin. Given its proclaimed use of self-interest to advance the interests of all, capitalism generally gets higher marks from those who stress the power of sin than does socialism, which assumes that humans suppress their private interests in the name of solidarity. Whether or not we accept this analysis of the place of sin in evaluating economic policy generally, it is quite alien to the Pastoral. Sin gets only brief notice in the discussion of scripture and only one mention amid the articulation of ethical principles. There the discussion sounds quite suggestive to Protestant ears:

> The Christian tradition recognizes, of course, that the fullness of love and community will be achieved only when God's work in Christ comes to completion in the kingdom of God. . . . Within history, knowledge of how to achieve the goal of social unity is limited. Human sin continues to wound the lives of both individuals and larger social bodies and places obstacles in the path toward greater social solidarity. If efforts to protect human dignity are to be effective, they must take these limits on knowledge and love into account. Nevertheless, sober realism should not be confused with resigned or cynical pessimism. (par. 67)

However, the bishops proceed immediately to their discussion of justice as participation in community. Sin is simply a theme left largely undeveloped in this document. Unless it plays a significant but unconscious function in shaping the policy positions of the bishops, it does not explain the discrepancy between principles and policies.

The bishops themselves certainly claim less authority for their policy recommendations:

> The soundness of our prudential judgments depends not only on the moral force of our principles, but also on the accuracy of our information and the validity of our assumptions.
>
> Our judgments and recommendations on specific economic issues, therefore, do not carry the same moral authority as our statements of universal moral principles and formal church teaching; the former are related to circumstances which can change or which can be interpreted differently by people of good will. (pars. 134-35)

At times this appears to be a matter of expertise. Bishops know Church teachings, and economists know economics. But far more commonly, the distinction between principles

137

and policies seems to be that of the more abstract, more permanent, and more absolute versus the more concrete, more changeable, and more relative. Yet this provides no good reason why the more abstract, permanent, and absolute principles are socialist while the more concrete, changeable, and relative are liberal capitalist. This is not to say that a great number of socialists have not found it necessary to be liberals to survive in the United States. However, the bishops certainly do not justify such compromise, and we should expect greater integrity from bishops than to compromise without at least a little rationalization.

Rethinking Moral Principles

The ears of most contemporary scholars of religion prick up whenever they hear the claim that any religious resource is absolute, unchanging, and authoritative. While the bishops note that the Catholic Church understands tradition to be continuing and changing, they do not finally treat either Scripture or the moral traditions to which they appeal as historical. The Scripture tells the story of people who lived at particular times and places marked by particular social institutions and cultural symbols. For instance, a people who still have a cultural memory of tribal life more easily speak of solidarity than a parishioner of a suburban congregation in the United States. The tribal heritage and monarchical political context are not incidental to the permanent message of the Hebrew Scriptures. They are why solidarity and community are central ethical categories, but they also heavily influence what those categories meant. Similarly, recognizing that this is the story of a minority group within a generally hostile Jewish and then Roman world is essential to understanding the emphasis on, and meaning of, solidarity in the New Testament. If we fail to recognize this historical context, and absolutize the religious resources arising from it, we raise historical contingencies to authoritative principles. This is what the bishops have done.

138

Similarly, the ethical framework presented in the Pastoral is a reworking of moral philosophy developed in a historical context where Church authority was much more clear and much more integrated with political and social authority. The social structure was also far more rigid and hierarchical. Once again, it is far easier to think in terms of solidarity and community in such a setting and even more possible to talk of the duties owed one to another. Moreover, solidarity and community mean quite different things in that context than in a modern democratic society.

These, however, are American bishops. They were not raised in a tribal, monarchical, or feudal world. Perhaps not, but they have been trained to believe, both formally and informally, that absolute truth came from just such social settings and that the contemporary world is marked by the alien values of gross individualism. They look backward with a certain ethically colored longing:

> Sustaining a common culture and a common commitment to moral values is not easy in our world. Modern economic life is based on a division of labor into specialized jobs and professions. . . . The benefits of this are evident in the satisfaction many people derive from contributing their specialized skills to society. But the costs are social fragmentation, a decline in seeing how one's work serves the whole community, and an increased emphasis on personal goals and private interests. This is vividly clear in discussions of economic justice. Here it is often difficult to find a common ground among people with different backgrounds and concerns. One of our chief hopes in writing this letter is to encourage and contribute to the development of this common ground. (par. 22)

Ironically, most historians of American religion would identify the period of greatest cultural unity and shared moral values with the Protestant dominance of the late nineteenth century. It was broken apart by waves of largely Catholic immigrants, a development many Protestants fought hard and long. Certainly few Americans, other than bishops, peer back beyond the industrial revolution with

139

much nostalgia. Yet the bishops are fundamentally correct; there was a certain solidarity and community that was lost.

Earlier, when he thought much differently, Michael Novak celebrated the Catholic enclaves for their resistance to melting into American culture. While his analysis was complex and controversial, he did argue for some basic distinctions in the Catholic subculture as opposed to the WASP culture, which speak to the issue at hand.[2] He identified the distinguishing characteristics of the Catholic perspective as loyalty—loyalty to family, clan, and community. One might even call this a sense of solidarity, although Novak clearly distinguishes it from the rational, mechanistic solidarity of the Marxist. It is marked by a basic respect for authority and an overriding focus on the immediate and local. While it may have its roots in a residual sense of the peasant who became the emigrant, this group solidarity has been deeply reinforced by WASP prejudice in the American setting. This most proximate root of the American bishops is in great continuity with the historical contexts of both the scriptural and moral resources to which they appeal. It is also in significant discontinuity with the upward mobility and relative lack of roots of many Catholics of the present generation.

All of these cultural settings—tribe, monarchy, feudalism, or American ethnic neighborhood—are quite different in both social organization and cultural values from contemporary pluralistic and individualistic America. These differences are well worth pointing out to those among us who think life has always been about "doing one's own thing." That does not make the old values authoritative politically, ethically, or religiously. What all of this does suggest is that the bishops may be much more conservative than they realize. They are attempting to preserve those institutions and values which have reinforced human fulfillment in the past. In that light, it is much easier to understand why the bishops, many of whom are quite the opposite of radical, can endorse a document dominated so thoroughly by appeals to solidarity and community. It also explains why they can then proceed to advocate such comparatively timid policy.

Three Solutions

Andrew Greeley has criticized the Pastoral for not being radical enough because it is not Catholic enough. In doing so he articulates one solution to the confusion we have identified. Recognize the Catholic view of organic society for what it is, a social theory not a religious absolute, then advocate that position strongly. Greeley suggests:

> Broadly speaking, there are four contending social theories that have been inherited from the late 18th century: capitalism and socialism believe in the centralization of power and decision-making and inattention to, if not out-right opposition toward, the working in the economy of the traditional social ties of family, friendship network, work group, local community and such "nonrational" ties as religion and ethnic group. Anarchism and Catholicism both rejected these two manifestations of bourgeois "liberalism" in favor of an economic order that is decentralized, pluralistic and organic in the sense that it is tied in with and respectful of the most intimate relationship networks of a person's life. Capitalism and socialism rejected the "corporate" society of late feudalism. Catholicism and anarchism advocated in opposition a return to the freedoms and protections of that decentralized, pluralistic and cooperative social order.[3]

By associating capitalism and socialism with bigness and Catholicism with pluralism, Greeley is already a long way into his advocacy position. Certainly, early capitalists thought they were escaping the limitations upon individual initiative built into the feudal order, and the pluralism of that order existed within a pretty rigid hierarchical structure.

What Greeley does quite convincingly is to distinguish the basic principles of Catholic social theory:

> It can be conveniently summarized under three principles—personalism, pluralism, and subsidiarity. Society exists for the

141

good of the person and not vice versa; that good is best served when power is held not by one social institution (the state) but by a wide variety of overlapping and crosscutting institutions; and (most important) the possession of power ought to be decentralized as much as possible.[4]

Although these principles are mixed somewhat with others and are never purely articulated in the pastoral, they consistently lie behind the moral position developed in it. This is the distinctively Catholic contribution to social theory, according to Greeley, and thus should have been the focus of the bishops' attention.

Second, Greeley identifies E. F. Schumacher as the best representative of this position in recent policy debates. This accurately labels Schumacher as a traditionalist. On this basis, Greeley contends that the bishops would have been much more true to their own principles if they had attacked bigness in both business and government as the overriding danger in the present U.S. economy. "Anyone steeped in the theory of the organic society . . . would suspect, almost a priori, that excessive size and unjustified concentration of power are its [American society's] most fundamental weaknesses and the most serious cause of both poverty and unemployment.[5] On the basis of this analysis, the bishops then should have advocated a radical restructuring of the entire society so that everything would be done on as small a scale as possible. Instead, the bishops merely endorsed "the fashionable liberalism of five years ago."[6] By missing the opportunity to be truly Catholic, the pastoral failed to be nearly as radical as it should have been.

The second solution is embodied in *Toward the Future*, the response to the pastoral published by a self-proclaimed Lay Commission. The Commission was dominated by conservative business people and academics. This lay letter claims to merge the best of the Catholic tradition with the best of the American. In fact, it reinterprets the Catholic tradition in terms of the American. By its telling, Catholic social thought can be reduced to three basic principles: "the dignity and uniqueness of every single human person; the social nature of human life; and the principle of subsidiarity."[7] While the bishops stress the social character of personhood, the Lay Commission describes their first principle in the language of self-reliance, individual responsibility, and liberty. Their characterization of the social nature stresses civic participation, pluralism, the universality of rights, and dissent. Finally, while the bishops appeal to subsidiarity in justifying federal assistance to local groups, the Lay Commission sees it as a rationale for localism and minimal government. Even in describing the Catholic moral tradition, the Lay Commission has begun to shift the emphasis toward what they see as essentially American.

The scale is tipped dramatically when the Commission lays out three American habits which it contends provide the means of practicing these Catholic principles. The three habits they discuss are: "the practice of free association; the habit of cooperation; and the underlying virtue of both, typically called by Americans 'the principle of self-interest rightly understood.' "[8] The Commission identifies free association primarily with business enterprises and charitable organizations. In tone, that discussion sounds much like the glorification of volunteerism so often a part of Ronald Reagan's picture of America. Cooperation is also considered primarily in terms of business enterprise. In both cases, the form of sociality celebrated is far from the descriptions of social settings, which form and shape humans for good or ill from birth, an idea that sits at the center of the bishops' analysis of human nature. The free independent individual precedes, then chooses to join, the voluntary associations and cooperative efforts portrayed in the lay letter.

The virtue appropriate to this individualism reaches its full expression in the principle of self-interest. According to the Lay Commission, self-interest is associated with sin. Thus, the Commission admits: "The American principle of self-interest rightly understood falls short of the full message of the Gospels. It is appropriate to a commonwealth of sinners.

143

While the Church has an obligation to encourage even heroic virtue, builders of political economy must be modest."[9] What follows, however, is much less begrudging allowance for original sin than a happy appreciation for the invisible hand of the market. The result eliminates any significant guilt we might feel for being self-interested: "The ancient dichotomy between self-interest and the common good has at the very least been diminished. To produce goods and services that make life better for others serves not only self-interest but the common good."[10] If, in fact, these three American habits put into practice what is essential to the Catholic tradition of social thought, the Enlightenment has finally won, at least in the United States. What we are left with is a portrayal of a liberal society composed of free individuals joining and cooperating in pursuit of their broad self-interest. Only now we are told it is actually Catholic, at least American Catholic.

What follows is quite predictable. The Lay Commission celebrates the virtues of entrepreneurship, compares American capitalism quite favorably with alternative systems, and responds to many criticisms of American business. Its policy recommendations tend to be moderately conservative. It supports the right of unions to organize and the need for some form of public assistance. However, it urges the serious consideration of free market alternatives and voluntary private charity over government programs. It is quite concerned that government efforts not drain too much money and talent from the private economy, thus stifling the source of vitality that is most likely to advance the common good.

Greeley urged the bishops to be Catholic; Novak and the Lay Commission pressed them to be American. I suppose I want them to be ecumenical, in a broad sense of that term. I agree with Michael Novak that the bishops should come to terms with the Enlightenment, but on its best terms, not its worst. Unlike Greeley, I think the bishops are right in rejecting, consciously or unconsciously, the alternative of attempting to return to a world that no longer is or can be,

144

except in the minds of such people as E. F. Schumacher. But if the bishops are to live in the modern world, they will need to bring their principles up to date, too. The alternative is the kind of confusion between principles and practice present in the pastoral as it stands. This means coming to terms once and for all with the Enlightenment—with individuality and pluralism.

The perspective developed in the last chapter drawing upon the thought of Hannah Arendt and Alfred North Whitehead does what the bishops need to do. It seeks to develop an integrated view of community and individuality which preserves the best of solidarity with the best of the Enlightenment. What is important to remember is the nature of individuality and the quality of community, which are valued by this perspective. It is not just the ability of the individual to choose that is prized, but the capacity to be creative and to add value. It is not just unity which is celebrated in community, but the harmonization of the richest diversity possible. This interplay between unique, creative individuality and diverse, pluralistic community is just what I find missing in the basic description of persons in the Pastoral. There are hints. The discussion of the dignity of humans which is expressed in their being created in the image of God is the closest the summary of Scripture comes. Expanded to relate the creative and valuing capacity in God and in humans, this section could lay solid groundwork for an adequate understanding of the human self. The exposition of rights also touches on this inherent dignity at points, but once again fails to ground these rights in the essential creative capacity of the self.

If such a view of the individual were developed in the pastoral, it would necessitate a much more dynamic and pluralistic view of community. This would correct what verges on a reductionist discussion of the social character of personhood and give new meaning to the terms community and solidarity. What we humans have in common is both the community we inherit and our creative capacity to shape the

145

future of that community toward higher value. Obviously, these are precisely the views of the individual and community developed at some length in the preceding chapter.

In writing of the contemporary United States, I have tended to associate the process social ethic with the political positions of Lester Thurow and Michael Harrington. Such positions take poverty and unemployment as central issues, not only because they involve human suffering, but also because they keep many people from making their creative contribution, thus impoverishing the community. They are highly suspicious of large corporations, not because they are big, but because they too often cut off creative possibilities for the many in pursuit of the interest of the few. They are thoroughly democratic because of the inherent dignity and importance of the individual.

There is very much in the pastoral which a Thurow or Harrington could support. However, it lacks the context and perspective a consistent rationale could provide. I believe that is because it has sanctified the social context out of which Scripture, Catholic moral tradition, and the American Catholic Church arose. Recognizing this context and taking seriously other contrary historical epochs, in this case the Enlightenment, opens up a broader and more adequate view of the human person in relation to human community. On this basis, more adequate, or at least better defended, moral principles and social policy are possible.

Notes

1. National Conference of Catholic Bishops, *Economic Justice for All* (Washington: United States Catholic Conference, 1986). It will be cited in the text by paragraph number.

2. Michael Novak, *The Rise of the Unmeltable Ethnics* (New York: Macmillan, 1971), pp. 46-48.

3. Andrew M. Greeley, "The Bishops and the Economy: A Radical Dissent," *America* 152 (January 12, 1986): 22. Reprinted with permission of America Press, Inc., 106 West 56th Street, New York, NY 10019. © 1985 All Rights Reserved.

4. Ibid., 22.

5. Ibid., 23.

6. Ibid., 24.

7. Lay Commission on Catholic Social Teaching and the U.S. Economy. *Toward the Future: Catholic Social Thought and the U.S. Economy: A Lay Letter* (New York: American Catholic Committee, 1984), p. 4.

8. Ibid., p. 17.

9. Ibid., p. 22.

10. Ibid., p. 23.

Chapter Eight

Reaganomics

As suggested in the introduction to this volume, Ronald Reagan brought with him to the White House the clearest commitment to conservative capitalist ideology of any president since the New Deal. However, it was the ideology of making money, not of protecting wealth accumulated in the past. He had come to wealth earlier in his life, and so had his friends. He was not the candidate of the Eastern established wealth but of the up and coming Western wealth. However, Reagan also arrived at the Presidency with the antagonism toward communism so characteristic of recent American conservatism. This was embodied most fully in his advocacy of dramatic increases in the military budget. On the way to the White House, Reagan picked up one final element of his ideological position—supply-side economics.

Supply-Side Theory

Supply-side economics traces its roots back to classical capitalist thought. As such it shares fully in Milton

Friedman's beliefs—individual liberty, the free market, and limited government. For such classical capitalists, the problem is always supply; that is, converting scarce resources to products people want. Demand is dependable; people will buy an attractive product at a price which offers a greater satisfaction than can be had if the same amount is spent elsewhere. This analysis was summarized in Say's Law of Markets, named for French physiocrat Jean Baptiste Say, who formulated it during the first half of the nineteenth century. According to Say's Law, money is but a medium of exchange which facilitates the barter of the goods I produce for those others produce. If I and others produce more, we can exchange more. Greater productivity creates greater demand, and thus is the key to economic growth.

None of this is foreign to other free-market capitalists. Neither is the next step in the supply-side analysis—that the present U.S. economy does not provide enough incentive and resources for increasing supply. The primary culprit is, of course, government. On the finance front, this means there is not enough investment in productivity, in technology, and in processes that will increase the supply of goods. On the personal income front, this means there is not enough incentive for people to work harder to increase the supply. As Reagan came to office, the most immediate target of these theses was the U.S. tax system.

Supply-side theorists argued that the tax system took too much money out of the economy that otherwise could go for investment purposes. They also contended that money was taken in the wrong way—by means of a progressive income tax which took such a high percentage of the next dollar to be earned by so many that it was not worth working hard to make that next dollar. The solution was obvious: reduce taxes and reduce progressivity. The projected result was that people would work harder and invest more, supply would grow, and everyone would be better off. So far Milton Friedman is on board. After all, he advocates a lower and flat tax.

It is at this point, however, that supply-side economics became controversial, even among free-market capitalists. Arthur Laffer, the best-known theorist of supply-side economics, began with a simple statistical reality.[1] Using the income tax as an example, a government can collect the same total revenue with a low tax on high incomes or a high tax on lower incomes. What has come to be called the Laffer Curve expresses this reality.[2]

THE LAFFER CURVE

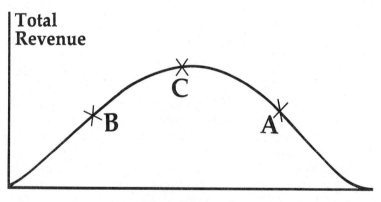

The revenue produced at point A at a high rate is the same as at point B, which is a lower rate.

151

Laffer made two further key assumptions. The first was that the United States government was then collecting a high tax on relatively low incomes. We were at point A on the curve. The second is that if that tax were reduced, our incomes would grow so that although we were paying a lower percentage in taxes, the actual revenue collected would be the same or more. Even Laffer would admit that it was not obvious just how much the tax rate could be cut before less revenue would be produced. He argued strongly that rates could be cut a lot without adversely affecting revenue except over a short transition period. In fact, if we set the tax rate at any point between A and B, such as at point C, revenue ought to increase.

Since they did not expect revenue to decline, true supply-side advocates did not stress the need for spending limitations in the way a Friedman does. This varied dramatically from the Republican orthodoxy which had always emphasized balanced budgets. In response, supply-siders contended that we could grow ourselves out of the budget deficit because growth would produce more revenue. Supply-siders also worried much less about restricting money supply. Increased production would take care of inflation and tight money only choke off the economic growth which the tax cut was stimulating. These deviations from traditional Republicanism explain most of the debate within the Reagan Administration over economic policy. The traditionalists urged budget cuts and tight money. The supply-siders showed relatively less concern about both.

Whether or not this makes economic sense is still under debate; that it made political sense is clear. Ronald Reagan came to the White House committed to cutting taxes and dramatically increasing military spending. Both were popular with the voters. A first set of budget cuts fell most heavily on those close to the poverty line, forcing many back down under that line. Then, Reagan ran into middle-class entitlement programs which he found he could not cut in the same ways because of political opposition. With the military budget up and domestic expenditures stable, the immediate loss in revenue from the tax cuts produced record deficits. Reagan would not cut military spending, would not raise taxes, and could not cut domestic spending further. Luckily, he had a theory that said none of those moves was necessary. He could just wait for the Laffer curve to come true as economic growth produced more tax revenue and reduced the deficit. How long could he wait? Certainly, until the 1984 election and perhaps until the end of his presidency. If it turned out Laffer was wrong, some future politicians would be left with the wreckage.

Reaganomics Enacted

The Reagan revolution erupted in 1981. All Reagan did in economic policy was propose what he had promised in the campaign—less taxes, higher military spending, less domestic spending, and less government regulation.[3] Actually, one key element in his economic policy was neither new nor revolutionary. Under Paul Volcker's leadership, the Federal Reserve had already instituted tighter monetary policy during the latter Carter years to bring down inflation. This continued under Reagan with considerable success in terms of inflation, but at the cost of the worst recession since the Great Depression. This recession and Reagan's popularity reached their bottoms in 1982.

The centerpiece of the Reagan revolution was the income tax cuts. True to supply-side theory and Reagan campaign rhetoric, these reductions were large and regressive. The President proposed that personal income tax rates be reduced by about one third but settled for closer to one fourth. Since the reductions in corporate taxes were much more complicated, the amount of the reduction was less clear, but was certainly more than that for individuals. Since the personal income tax cuts were mostly an across-the-board cut in the amount paid, it was most helpful to those who paid a large amount of taxes, the upper income

153

taxpayers. This follows supply-side theory since these persons were paying the highest rate on each new dollar of income (marginal rate), and thus had the least incentive to keep working harder. Since these persons also had more disposable income, they were more likely to invest part of their tax savings, thus helping increase supply. The cuts in corporate taxes were intended to free up more money for investment in productivity even more directly. They were skewed toward the newer higher productivity industries rather than the older established ones. This reflected supply-side theory, Reagan's personal experience, and the geography of his political constituency (Southern and Western).

Fresh from victory on taxes, Reagan moved on to the budget. Here his convictions were clear but in conflict. As a conservative he was committed to shrinking the size of government, but as an anti-Communist he was committed to matching and surpassing the Soviets in the arms race. The only solution was to slash domestic spending and to increase military spending dramatically. In total fiscal impact, these contrary movements tended to cancel out each other.

As one who had run against welfare for years, Reagan took on the domestic budget cutting with great relish. That enthusiasm was limited a bit by his desire not to look too mean. Rhetorically, this was solved through use of the phrases "preserving the safety net" and "assisting the truly needy." In practice, this meant that the budget cuts focused not on the very poor but on the barely poor and the nearly poor. These families had been made eligible for food stamps, medical benefits, job training assistance, and so forth, as much by Nixon reforms as by Democratic ones because they were the working poor, implying the deserving poor. Now they were eliminated from those programs because they were the not truly needy. The President basically won the first round of domestic budget cuts.

At this point he ran into trouble on the domestic front. Surrounded by media coverage of the food kitchens and the homeless, which were both growing because of the recession, Congress was not willing to cut assistance to the poor much more. The largest sources for new reductions were programs which served, or at least included, the middle class, such as social security, veteran benefits, college loans, and agricultural supports. This is the story David Stockman tells so well.[4] Congress balked at these cuts. After they felt Democrats used Reagan's proposed changes in Social Security to defeat Republicans in the 1982 election, Republicans inside and outside the Administration also lost their enthusiasm for going after these entitlement programs. That left relatively little domestic spending to debate.

At the same time, the combination of tax cuts and the deep recession of 1981–82 had cut revenues so much that the deficit became a major issue. The result was a compromise package of budget reduction and tax increases. Reagan saved his supply-side face by arguing that the tax increases were merely revenue enhancements, which were the necessary price for further budget cuts and by declaring the personal income tax rates untouchable. True believers in the supply side theory denounced this as the "unraveling of Reaganomics."[5] After that time, the fiscal story became boringly repetitive. Each year the President looked to slice a little more out of domestic spending, while the Democrats in the House tried to hold back the increases in military spending. The Senate Republicans sought some compromise between these two as well as a little movement from the President on small tax increases and even some minimal raids on the entitlements. The basic result was stalemate with President Reagan getting a little out of domestic spending and the Congress slowing the growth in the military budget somewhat. And the budget deficits grew.

In a sense, this is enough of the story of Reagan economic policy. The major changes were enacted in 1981 and one major adjustment occurred in 1982. The stalemate that followed and its product, Gramm-Rudman, were not a part of the Reagan revolution so much as results of it. What

155

other results did it bring? In terms of economic growth, an extremely deep recession was followed by the expectable recovery, then slow growth. In inflation, tight money aided by low prices in commodities, especially oil and agricultural products, brought prices down dramatically. In deficits, those of the federal government and of trade grew immensely. This is all clear and beyond controversy. The deeper meaning of Reaganomics is open to much more debate. Who better to debate that matter than our old friends—Milton Friedman, Lester Thurow, and Michael Harrington.

Friedman

As already suggested, Friedman basically agreed with Reagan's program. This included supply-side economics, although his endorsement was interesting both for what it said and for the misgivings it suggested. He did not believe that supply-side economics was new. It was just a new name for policies, which some of those using the new name had oversold. He concluded: "The essence of supply-side economics is simply good economic analysis. It's simply the elementary proposition that people will move in the direction that promises higher rewards and will leave activities that promise lower rewards."[6] With these words, Friedman basically blessed supply-side economics as but a new name for the free market capitalism of which he has become a symbol.

In fact, Friedman agreed even more with Reagan's full economic program than with the more rabid fans of supply-side economics. He summed up his position with his usual definiteness:

> During his campaign in 1980, President Reagan outlined a four-point program that he regarded as required to get the economy back on a good path. . . : lower government spending, lower government marginal tax rates, less government regulation, a steady and moderate rate of monetary

growth. These are the four keys to success, and nothing else will do it. All other proposals are smoke screens.[7]

Taken together, what this program came to was less government and more free market, which we know is Friedman's basic position. If Friedman, himself, had been elected President, this would have been his program.

Friedman doubted the projections of the true believers in supply-side economics, which showed revenue increasing from the tax cuts. Given his basic goal of less government, if these projections did prove true it would only be cause to cut taxes further. As a monetarist, Friedman was not particularly concerned about the economic impact of deficits anyway. However, he did consider them very effective political tools. By cutting taxes and producing a deficit, Reagan forced Congress to cut expenditures, and the entire political discussion turned to the deficits and how to control them. In this climate, the size of government might shrink; at least it should not grow as fast as it had in the past. Thus, Friedman supported tax cuts not as a way to increase revenue but as a step toward less government.

In fact his primary concerns were that the Reagan economic program did not go far enough toward Reagan's own goals and that it was not permanent. By Friedman's calculations, the major cut in income taxes was largely cancelled out by increases in the social security tax so the overall level of taxation remained relatively constant.[8] At the same time, spending continued to grow. The largest area of increase was in military spending. The second largest was what he called middleclass welfare—Social Security, Medicare, and other retirement programs. The third significant area he mentioned are those programs that grow during recessions, such as unemployment compensation and agricultural supports. The only substantial cuts he saw were in programs run by state and local government, including education, training and employment transportation, community development, and revenue sharing. Welfare programs for the poor remained constant.[9] He summed it all up in these words: "The Reagan years have seen a start toward achieving President Reagan's objective of cutting tax rates. They have seen no progress toward his parallel objectives."[10]

Friedman's explanation for this fairly minimal success is the great momentum in growth that government had developed prior to 1980 and the resistance of what he calls the iron triangle of beneficiaries, politicians, and bureaucrats. The only two sources of defense against this iron triangle for the average citizen are the Presidency and the Constitution. Writing in 1983, Friedman hoped Reagan would win reelection in 1984, and then use the brief honeymoon period which followed to push his basic goals further. The only permanent solution is a constitutional amendment which limits taxes and spending to a certain percentage of national income. The primary lesson Friedman distilled from the Reagan experiment was that even a strong president with the right program needs the help of the Constitution to battle the iron triangle successfully.[11]

Thurow

As we should fully expect from what we know of Thurow, he shares none of Friedman's enthusiasm for Reaganomics. He boils Reaganomics down to two things, monetarism and supply-side economics, and concludes that neither worked. By his telling, the result of the tight monetary policy was the major recession of 1981–82. He says that this strategy died on August 13, 1982. On that date the Reagan administration decided to lend Mexico the billions of dollars it needed in order not to default on its loans from American banks. This prevented a possible financial panic, but also pumped those billions into the U.S. money supply as Mexico paid the banks over the following twelve months. The prime interest rate fell from 15.5 percent to 10.5 percent over that period. Thurow summarized: "What had been a policy of slow monetary growth was reborn as a policy of rapid monetary growth."[12]

The death of supply-side economics took much longer. Remember that the theory of supply-side economics is that a reduction in marginal tax rates will encourage people to work harder and save more. The resulting increased work effort and investment is supposed to increase productivity, and therefore economic growth and tax revenues. During the four years of the Carter administration, the personal savings rate was 6 percent, only half of that of the rest of the industrialized world. In 1983, when the tax cuts were in effect, the rate dropped to 5 percent; it rose back to 6.1 percent in 1984. "When it came to the bottom line, Americans of all income classes were spenders, not savers."[13]

This consumption converted supply-side economics into demand-side economics. Instead of investment pulling the economy into greater productivity and growth, demand pushed the economy into expansion. Government followed the lead of the private consumers, increasing its spending by 39 percent between 1981 and 1984, including a doubling of the defense budget. And the federal deficit rose. Thurow's overall conclusion was:

> Although it was never publicly admitted, the Reagan Administration had become "born again Keynesians," converted to easy money, large tax cuts, big increases in government spending, and huge deficits. Midway through his first term of office President Reagan had adopted precisely the policies which he spent a lifetime denouncing.[14]

As a modified Keynesian himself, Thurow thought these policies were quite right for an economy in deep recession in 1982.

However, as the U.S. economy recovered from the recession during 1983 and 1984, Thurow saw two major danger signs and a lingering fundamental problem. After a slight increase typical of periods of economic recovery, productivity became stagnant again in 1984 and 1985. Remember Thurow's insistence that the only real basis for long-term economic growth and higher standards of living is greater productivity. The alternative is a continual trade-off between high inflation and high unemployment.

Writing in 1985, Thurow contended that the reason we did not see this fundamental problem of productivity was that we had postponed its effects. This brings us to the two danger signs. The first was the trade deficit which had grown precipitously. When tight money policies pushed interest rates up in the United States, foreign investors moved their funds here, forcing up the value of the dollar. Then, when the U.S. economy began to grow more quickly than the world economy, we bought more than we sold. This produced a trade deficit. In free market theory, this should have led to a drop in the value of the dollar, but that did not happen for some time. Thus, U.S. firms were still unable to sell as much as we bought, but we paid for this trade deficit (and also for part of our Federal deficit) by borrowing from foreigners. Sooner or later, Thurow was certain that the value of the dollar would come down, and we would have to pay back those debts. A decline in the value of the dollar would show up as inflation because foreign goods would then cost more. Repayment of the debts would simply require us to sacrifice some of our standard of living in order to pay up. Thurow summed up: "To preserve today's standard of living Americans are literally mortgaging tomorrow's standard of living."[15]

A federal deficit is a negative public savings rate, just as my auto loan represents negative personal savings. For the entire economy the result is the same, too. If we all (including the Federal government) borrow in order to consume, less money is left to invest. Less investment means productivity does not increase, and we become even less able to compete with other nations who are saving and investing much more than we are. Inevitably, if slowly, our standard of living declines. Once again, we are sacrificing future improvements in our standard of living in order to finance present consumption.

160

Thurow pulled this whole discussion together in this pessimistic conclusion:

> Americans are now enjoying the calm in the eye of the hurricane. They have not entered an era of permanent prosperity. A maxi-recession is behind them, they are now enjoying current prosperity, but ahead of them lie some difficult times. Neither the balance of payments nor the Federal budget can forever remain in deficit. Inflation will not remain as somnolent as it now is. Unemployment hovers at unacceptable levels. The secrets of productivity growth remain elusive.[16]

In sum, the basic problem of making the U.S. economy competitive in the world seemed just as real to Thurow after five years of Reagan as it did in 1980 when *The Zero-Sum Society* appeared. All that had changed was that much of the future of the U.S. economy had been mortgaged in the meantime.

As we saw earlier, Thurow's interest in economic growth is fueled in the final analysis by his commitment to equality. In his opinion, there was actual retrogression on that front during the Reagan years. The decline of U.S. industry undercut the American middle class as workers traded well-paying industrial jobs for low-paying work or unemployment. At the same time, the Reagan administration shifted income from poor and near poor to the well-off through conscious policy choices, especially the tax and spending cuts. Thurow believed this was unjustified, even on Reagan's own terms, increasing productivity: "Fortunately the changes that will be necessary to make the economy more efficient are congruent with what needs to be done to make the economy more equitable. In this case efficiency and equity go together."[17] For Thurow, although welfare had a role to play, jobs remained the key.

Harrington

Harrington's evaluation of Reaganomics was not all that different from Thurow's. As usual, however, he drew much more radical lessons from what he saw as its failure. He, too, described the 1981–82 recession as the natural consequence of tight monetary policy and the 1983–84 recovery as a tribute to Keynesian demand-side economics. He pushed his conclusion further:

> Even though Reagan's Economic Recovery Act of 1981 cheapened capital and subsidized savings, it was followed by an investment bust and a decline in savings. The problem, it turned out, was not a lack of investment funds but the structure of a chronically malfunctioning economy.[18]

Like Thurow, then, Harrington considered the recovery of 1983–84 just a brief break from a lingering crisis in the U.S. economy: "Reaganomics . . . has purchased at intolerable cost a temporary recovery; the mounting deficit and continued high unemployment make it highly probable that the crisis will resume."[19]

Partially in laying groundwork for his own position, Harrington characterized the Reagan program as planned government intervention rather than as the unfettered free market. In relation to inflation for instance, Harrington charged:

> Reagan has his way of fighting inflation. It's supposedly "no-hands"—the Government does nothing. That's utter nonsense. The Reagan method involved a heavy use of governmental powers, through monetarism and other policies, to disemploy about 12 million Americans. Their unemployment did buy us lower prices. That is one way. You can roast the pig by burning down the barn.[20]

Similarly, the Reagan tax cuts were intended to establish certain incentives and disincentives for individual choices on savings and investment. Reaganomics was government planning "which established a framework within which decisions were to be made, primarily through tax laws and then channeled money to those assumed most likely to invest, the rich."[21] In a sense, we got the worst of both worlds, government planning followed by private decision-making by the wealthy and powerful.

One major result of Reaganomics, according to Harrington, was the inequality Thurow described. However, Harrington called it division between the rich and the poor. By conscious policy choices, the Reagan administration cut the programs that supported the working poor and the taxes of the wealthy. Partly through policy choices and partly by simply allowing the tendencies of corporate capitalism in the '80s to run their course, the administration undermined the American middle class. The result was the emergence of a dual economy as blue collar industrial workers fell from the middle class. Harrington concluded:

> The occupational shifts described here lead to an entrenched dual economy. This dual economy persists despite the current recovery. The old liberal wisdom—that in the long run the private economy will generate new and better jobs, and that this is the only real solution to poverty—becomes less and less relevant. An occupational structure characterized by a polarization between high paid professional and technical workers on the one hand and poorly paid, unorganized, lower-level workers on the other will be threatened, not by revolution, but by social demoralization and/or constant outbreaks of individual, nihilistic violence.[22]

To be clear, Harrington recognized that much of this deterioration in the status of blue-collar workers was tied to technology and the internationalization of the economy rather than just Reagan. However, he considered this but further proof of his thesis that the problem lies with the very structure of corporate capitalism.

The identification of this problem as a dual economy reminds us that Harrington's final ethical principle is solidarity. A dual economy is wrong because it divides the community. His prescription remained the same also. In place of the corporate planning of the managed economy under Reagan, he proposed decentralized, democratic

163

planning. The overall goal remained the same, full employment. One particular target was even more clear, the preservation and revitalization of the industrial heart of the United States. The final purpose was consistent, the establishing of solidarity among citizens of the United States and the world at large. While Harrington recognized that all of this seemed out of tune with the public mood of the Reagan years, he remained convinced Reagan's policies would aggravate the economic crisis. Then more radical policy options would be possible.

Reaganomics on Balance

In the terms of our discussion of informing ethical principles, Reaganomics was a strong assertion of liberty. Reagan's most direct statement of this principle was his question of voters during the 1984 election: "Are you better off now than you were four years ago?" This certainly was not self-transcendent liberty. Rather, it was a direct appeal to the most elemental form of self-interest. Indeed, particularly in his appeals to the religious right, Reagan seemed quite prepared to trample on the individual rights of everyone from pregnant women to school children, from gays to workers, and from readers of *Playboy* to welfare recipients. The most that can be said in his defense on these counts is that he failed to enact legislation in most of these areas. Whether the judges he appointed accomplish the same goals by a different means is yet to be seen. In any event, Reagan's view of liberty surely favored greed over free expression.

If we entered the Reagan years with one of the worst records in establishing equality in the industrial world, matters got much worse. The distribution of both income and wealth became more unequal. Poverty increased, and the middle class declined. This was justified primarily by the hope that renewed economic growth would improve everyone's standard of living, but that has yet to happen. Reagan attacked, and to a significant extent stymied, programs aimed directly at equality, such as affirmative action. Affirmative action assumes that the self is related and that some of us received a head start in the race of life because we were white males. Affirmative action seeks to overcome that head start so that we all have equal opportunity. In the name of individual liberty, the Reagan administration came to the defense of white males who lost out because of affirmative action. If we are but independent agents, the administration was correct. If we are a product of our past and present relationships to a significant extent, affirmative action is justified and the administration's position was principled and wrong.

As for solidarity, Reagan was given credit for unifying America once more and giving us a sense of restored pride in ourselves. Yet beneath the surface divisions grew. Black Americans consistently perceived Reagan as antagonistic to their purposes as reflected in the huge majority of blacks voting against Reagan in the face of the 1984 landslide. The gap between urban and suburban schools did not shrink. Programs designed to bring the poor into the mainstream of the economy were decimated by the Reagan budget cuts. Once Reagan set the stage for union busting with his treatment of the air controllers, organized labor was forced out of fear and despair to give up past gains and abandon a good number of their members. Entire regions, especially the rural and the industrial middle of the country, felt separated from the relatively well-off coastal areas. While President Reagan appeared to have restored patriotism based on a militaristic nationalism and largely unrealized hopes for general prosperity, divisions among Americans grew.

If, as I argued in chapter 5, the United States needs more equality and solidarity, Ronald Reagan did not bring it. We remain an unequal and divided society. Indeed, Reagan was not even true to the best of his own guiding principle, liberty. Rather, we have seen the extension of a society and economy based on greed. Yet this should not surprise us. Free-market

165

theory claims that self-interest will drive an economy to greater efficiency and growth. Has it? Did Reaganomics, antagonistic to equality and solidarity as it was, work economically?

In certain ways it surely did. Tight money worked. It brought down inflation at the cost of the worst recession since the Great Depression. This was not surprising to most economists, who disagree less about the likelihood this would happen than they do about whether the cost was worth it. Price collapses in energy and food helped hold overall prices down. The underlying inflation rate promised to recover in time requiring us to face the issue of the relative value of stable prices or recession once again. After 1982, relaxed monetary policy and an extremely stimulatory fiscal policy fueled by tax cuts, rapid military spending and deficits led to a strong recovery. Again economists were not surprised and disagreed only over precisely why it occurred and how long it would last.

As the recovery leveled off, certain realities became clear. At its best the economy seemed incapable of reducing the unemployment rate much below 5 percent. Even allowing for some changes in the nature of the work force, when combined with the number of persons who have given up looking for work, who work part-time, or who work in low paying deadend jobs, this constitutes a major national problem. The problem is compounded by the fact that it is concentrated in minority groups and in particular geographic locales. Moreover, the implications of such levels of unemployment are much broader than generally recognized. For instance, it is hard to see any solution to the crisis of the poor minority family as long as unemployment for marriage age minority men is around fifty percent in many urban areas. Failure to reduce unemployment further does not bode well for either equality or solidarity as Thurow and Harrington clearly indicate.

After some expected improvement during the early part of the recovery, productivity also leveled off. As a result we are

166

only somewhat better able to compete in world markets.[23] This coupled with slower growth among our major trading partners means we continue to buy more than we sell, and our trade deficit and debt to other countries grow. Even a dramatic decline in the value of the dollar by the end of the Reagan years only brought modest improvement in the trade deficit. At a minimum, there is little evidence that the Reagan tax cut spurred greater work effort and more investment in productivity. Rather, there seems every reason to conclude with Thurow that we do not have our competitive house in order, that we still are unable to compete internationally. Perhaps the most obvious proof of this is the renewed pressure for protectionism.

Finally, there is the sense that what Reagan accomplished ideologically was to box in the liberals. The budget debates were all overshadowed by the deficit. Liberals could attempt to protect social spending and cut defense. Conservatives could try to protect defense and cut social spending. Neither seemed willing to take on social security or raise taxes without the support of a President. No one dared consider new expenditures unless it was a little money for drug enforcement. In addition, the liberal response in the past to a downturn in the economy had been Keynesian stimulus. In the face of $200 billion deficits, talking about more tax cuts or increases in expenditures was politically impossible. Reagan used up the Keynesian resources and did not replenish them.

Reaganomics did not succeed on its own terms. A redirection in inflation was bought with a deep recession and a lot of luck in commodity prices. The recovery was driven by Keynesian demand-side growth. The supply-side revolution in productivity did not materialize, unemployment ran high, and the trade deficit grew. The ethical price paid for this mixed economic performance is the dignification of greed, greater inequality, and expanding fundamental division in our society. It is time to consider alternatives.

Notes

1. Arthur B. Laffer, "Government Exactions and Revenue Deficiencies" in Bruce Bartlett and Timothy P. Roth (eds.), *The Supply-Side Solution* (Chatham, N.J.: Chatham House Publishers, 1983), pp. 120-39, or in Richard H. Fink (ed.), *Supply-Side Economics: A Critical Appraisal* (Frederick, Md.: University Publications of America, 1982), pp. 185-203.

2. The Laffer Curve was published in *Foundations of Supply-Side Economics*, Victor A. Canto, Douglas H. Joines, and Arthur B. Laffer (New York: Academic Press, 1983), p. 9.

3. Summaries of the Reagan program similar to this are given by both advocate Bruce R. Bartlett, *Reaganomics: Supply-Side Economics in Action* (New York: Quill, 1982), p. 211, and critics John L. Palmer and Isabel V. Sawhill, "Perspectives on the Reagan Experiment" in Palmer and Sawhill (eds.), *The Reagan Experiment* (Washington, D.C.: Urban Institute Press, 1982), pp. 4-10.

4. William Greider, "The Education of David Stockman," *The Atlantic Monthly* 248 (December 1981): 27-54. Stockman's own version of the Reagan revolution is described on pages 29 and 30.

5. Paul Craig Roberts, *The Supply-Side Revolution* (Cambridge, Mass.: Harvard University Press, 1984), p. 226.

6. Milton Friedman, "Supply-Side Policies: Where Do We Go from Here?" in Federal Reserve Bank of Atlanta and Emory University Law and Economics Center, *Supply-Side Economics in the 1980s* (Westport, Conn.: Quorum Books, 1982), pp. 53-54.

7. Ibid., p. 59.

8. Milton and Rose Friedman, *Tyranny of the Status Quo* (New York: Harcourt Brace Jovanovich, 1984), pp. 29-30.

9. Ibid., pp. 30-33.

10. Ibid., p. 34.

11. Ibid., pp. 165-68.

12. Lester C. Thurow, *The Zero-Sum Solution* (New York: Simon and Schuster, 1985), p. 29.

13. Ibid., p. 30.

14. Ibid.

15. Ibid., p. 36.

16. Ibid., p. 44.

17. Ibid., p. 115.

18. Michael Harrington, "If There Is a Recession—and If Not," *Dissent* 32 (Spring 1985): 140.

19. Michael Harrington and Irving Howe, "Voices from the Left: A Conversation Between Michael Harrington and Irving Howe," *New York Times Magazine* 133 (June 17, 1984): 32.

20. Ibid., p. 34.

21. Michael Harrington, "A Path for America," *Dissent* 29 (Fall 1982): 411.

22. Michael Harrington, "The Perils of a Dual Economy," *Dissent* 32 (Fall 1985): 426.

23. As we shall see in the next chapter, just how able the United States is to compete and under what conditions is a matter of considerable debate among economists.

Chapter Nine

Alternatives for the Future

As a political rallying point, Reaganomics died on October 19, 1987. Regardless of its economic significance, the stock market crash established that. Indeed, most economists (including Friedman and Thurow) downplay its economic importance. The immediate threat was to the financial system. In 1930 that system responded poorly and further collapse followed; this time the Federal Reserve responded quickly and the system seems to have weathered the storm. Thurow actually believes that the long-term effect may be positive because it forced the Federal Reserve to lower interest rates to support the economy instead of raising them to protect the dollar as it was doing before the crash. Since the Fed's postcrash policy is what he advocated all along, he is encouraged.[1]

The standard evaluation of those we have been analyzing was that nothing truly significant was changed by the events of October 19, 1987. Milton Friedman believes government remains too large. Lester Thurow and his fellow neoliberal Robert Reich believe the problem of competitiveness remains. As Reich put it:

The economic "crisis" that Wall Street tells us we have just experienced is, in fact, no different from the slowly gathering crisis that existed before October 19. The real economy had been unraveling for years while America busily consumed more than it produced . . .

What we need to do now is what we should have been doing all along.[2]

Harrington believes that fault still lies in the structure of capitalism. What was changed by the stock crash and the continuing fall in the value of the dollar was Americans' confidence in Reaganomics. After October 19, 1987, critics of Reagan's policies from the right and from the left could get a much greater hearing than before.

Critics from the Right

Many of the supporters of Reaganomics believe it is an excellent idea which has not been fully tried yet. Supply-siders argue that taxes have not actually gone down very much. They complain that when they are coupled with increases in the Social Security tax and state and local taxes, the tax increases pushed through by Congress in 1982 all but cancelled out the positive effects of the 1981 income tax cuts. Furthermore, restrictive monetary policy handicapped the early returns from the 1981 cuts, and the anti-corporate bias of the 1986 tax reform package which hurt investment then, shut off some of the later possibilities. All in all, true supply-side policies have never been fully put to test, and a cut in overall taxation is still in order.

Milton Friedman would agree with most of these general observations, but propose a different solution. President Reagan forced big spenders to talk about deficit reduction. Yet action did not follow. What is still needed is a constitutional amendment which requires a balanced budget or preferably sets limits on what percentage of the national income the Federal Government can tax and spend. This not only would force government to shrink in size, but also would limit future growth to the amount the economy grows.

The voice of the purists can be heard in both of these critiques. Since theories seldom get enacted in just the form proposed, their advocates nearly always complain that their ideas would have worked if they had not been compromised. Both the supply-siders and Friedman can celebrate the reduction of marginal tax rates and of domestic spending other than entitlements like Social Security. Yet this merely symbolizes the fact that the pure practice of either theory would merely accentuate the increased inequality and social division which Reaganomics has already brought. Absent any clear indication that either of these pure alternatives would deliver the economic growth they promise, the high ethical price they would exact is hard to justify.

Neo-conservatism is finally a defense of traditional mainstream American values against the imagined attack of the alienated—radical minorities, feminists, students, and professors. It had a certain cohesion when all it opposed seemed on the rise, but in the America of Ronald Reagan that apparent unity has unraveled. The religious right focuses on pornography and abortion and prayer, instead of evolution in schools. While it endorses the free market, it neither knows nor cares about specific economic and social policy. The more sophisticated neo-conservatives have been forced by Reagan to choose between free market and liberal capitalism. Michael Novak and Irving Kirstol have chosen to become apologists for corporate capitalism. They retain some overtones of social responsibility, but have thrown their lot in with Reagan. On the other hand, Daniel Moynihan has returned to the New Deal Democrat fold. Once again, he argues for full employment and family support to counter the collapse of poor families. All in all, there is no need to analyze a neo-conservative view of the economy as a separate position in the debate.

Options to the Left

On the left are three main contenders for our economic future—traditional Keynesianism, neo-liberalism, and democratic socialism. Part of the difference among these three positions is factual. Just how much of the balance-of-trade problem could be solved by a fall in the value of the dollar? However, they also represent gradations of emphasis upon equality and community. Just how the factual determinations and the value commitments interact is difficult to determine very precisely.

Traditional Keynesianism

Is the United States becoming a nation of hamburger stands? This is the question Robert Z. Lawrence, a key proponent of the traditional Keynesian analysis, addresses in his Brookings publication entitled *Can America Compete?*[3] As I indicated in chapter 3, traditional Keynesians share Lester Thurow's basic ethical commitment to equality. Where they differ with him is in their judgment about the basic health of American industry. Lawrence challenges many of the assumptions he believes conservatives and many liberals share about the U.S. economy. The manufacturing sector of the domestic economy is shifting, but continues to grow. Research and development expenditures by American industries have not declined in recent years, raising serious questions about increased investment as the solution to our productivity problems. Lawrence concludes that the U.S. economy is not deindustrializing, nor are imports forcing such deindustrializing upon us.

The shadow of Keynes falls across both his judgments about what the real cause of our problems is and his prescriptions. He locates the primary blame for our poor economic performance in misguided domestic macroeconomic policy. For instance, the decline in basic industries, such as auto and steel, flowed primarily from weak domestic

174

demand, not from foreign competition. Furthermore, the decision to run a large deficit in the Federal budget financed to a significant extent by foreign loans resulted in demand being shifted to the United States from other countries. Goods follow demand. Since the United States was doing the buying, in part with foreign funds, foreign firms naturally were doing their selling here rather than at home where demand was down, in part because funds had been shipped to the United States. U.S. exporters also found a smaller demand for their goods abroad. In Lawrence's view, this led naturally to a strong dollar. What a weaker dollar will do is not yet clear.

The solutions, then, are consistent full-employment macroeconomic policies. The immediate goals of such policy is to stabilize domestic demand, to reduce the full-employment deficit, and to bring down the value of the dollar. Not only would this solve most of our competitive problems, but it would also establish the framework essential to the success of any programs designed to improve the competitive capacity of particular industries. He warns: "In the absence of a shift in macroeconomic policies, selective industrial policies may change the composition of the trade balance and employment but are unlikely to affect their aggregate levels."[4]

Lawrence is skeptical of any policy that seeks to make structural changes in the economy. In particular, he doubts that any planning agency would be better than the market at making basic decisions about where best to allocate resources. He aims specific criticism at approaches which target an entire industry because, in nearly every case, the problem varies so much from firm to firm as to defy lumping them together. Lawrence thinks this illustrates a broader rule: "Many U.S. structural and trade policies could be improved but the flaws in industry-wide targeting point to a superior approach—confine government intervention to clear cases of market failure in which policies have a reasonable chance of improving market performance; when intervening, ensure that policies are targeted to remedy market failure as precisely as possible."[5]

If this sounds a bit like Friedman, that is not accidental. Yet, Lawrence recognizes a much larger number of market failures than Friedman would. For instance, he advocates much more generous provision of student loans and much broader government support for both basic research and industrial research and development, including tax incentives, direct subsidies and even government operated research. He even advocates establishing a government agency to gather information about, and analyze the effects of, government assistance to industries and firms.[6] However, in the final analysis, Lawrence is clearly a reformed capitalist with the emphasis on the market:

> The call for greater government intervention, on the grounds that it would make U.S. industry more farsighted, is ironic. For a world in which governments bail out private firms that fail to adapt is one that rewards myopic and static behavior. Even in a world in which some U.S. government response to actions of foreign governments is required, policy-makers should not lose sight of what is the exception and what is the rule. The best rule for the United States is still to let the market allocate.[7]

Government needs to set the appropriate macroeconomic climate and respond to market failures, but individual decisions guided by market conditions remain far preferable to any public planning process.

The Neo-Liberals

As neo-liberals, Lester Thurow and Robert Reich[8] see problems in the structure of the U.S. economy which will require more than just helping the market work. Thurow responds directly to Lawrence by agreeing, on the one hand, that more stable, full-employment macroeconomic policies are essential.[9] On the other hand, Thurow contends that Lawrence's conclusion that the United States can compete is based on the acceptance of a falling dollar. Given this assumption, the United States can compete, but it will be competition based on falling wages and a declining standard of living. Thurow concludes:

> To accept a falling dollar as a solution to America's competitiveness problem is to accept an economy that competes on the basis of low wages and not higher productivity. . . . The economy is technically competitive and has achieved a balance in its balance of payments, but when Americans say that they want to be competitive they are saying something quite different. They are saying that they want to compete based on efficiency and innovation and a standard of living second to none.[10]

Reich and Thurow are convinced that we cannot compete on these terms without some basic changes in our institutional policy structure.

We have already considered Thurow's proposals in some detail. At the core of Reich's analysis is the thesis that production is increasingly shifting from the mass industrial style to more flexible processes which require highly skilled workers turning out high technology products precisely fitted to particular uses. To navigate this transition successfully, the United States must increase its investments in human capital, while shifting to a more cooperative and decentralized industrial and governmental structure. To be accepted these measures must be seen as equitable. The costs must be distributed fairly. This leads Reich to propose grants to industries to lure the hard to employ, subsidies for workers caught in the transition, and loans for job training. To stimulate technological advances, he advocates Federal support for research, regional development banks, investment councils composed of bankers and government and labor, and broader worker participation in managing firms.

Although there is some disagreement upon details, Thurow and Reich clearly agree on the broad direction policy should head. Both insist on the need to expand and focus research and development and investment in high technology

177

areas. Both stress the centrality of human capital, meaning education and job skills, in the economy to come. Both insist that there not only is no trade-off between equality and efficiency, but that greater equality is essential to the transition which must take place.

Of particular importance to the issues we have raised in this volume, Reich and Thurow, especially in his most recent works, draw upon the value of community as well as that of equality. In *The Next American Frontier*, Reich pulls them both together in these terms:

> The central theme of this book is that in the emerging era of productivity, social justice is not incompatible with economic growth, but essential to it. A social organization premised on equity, security and participation will generate greater productivity than one premised on greed and fear. Collaboration and collective adaptation are coming to be more important to an industrialized nation's well being than are personal daring and ambition.[11]

Indeed the very model of the productive process which Reich believes is becoming dominant, especially in high-technology and high-productivity firms, is one that stresses cooperative and flexible team effort. Not surprisingly, cultures which traditionally have emphasized community, such as those of Asia, are adapting well to such processes. We would do well to put our highly structured and conflictual institutions behind us if we are to compete in world markets.

In fact, Thurow argues that our Lone Ranger image of economic success is largely a myth. In reality, the genius of the greater heroes of our industrial history, such as Henry Ford, was their capacity to get people to work together.[12] Like Reich, Thurow concludes:

> Since economies are almost by definition social organizations, it is not surprising the economic genius almost always involves the ability to organize a society better; but any society that insists on describing its own history as if it were a product of rugged individuals and nothing else is apt to underestimate the

importance of social organization. . . . And if there has ever been a society that has fallen into this trap, it is America.[13]

This recent emphasis on community in Thurow's writing seems to parallel his study of the Japanese economy. This should be of some concern to those committed to a dynamic, pluralistic community since the Japanese practice of community is often quite rigid and hierarchical. Indeed, it may have much in common with the view of community we saw in the traditional Roman Catholicism represented in the U.S. bishops pastoral letter on the economy.[14] In rejecting a static and constricted view of individuality we must guard against adopting an equally limited view of community.

Democratic Socialism

Writing in 1980, Lester Thurow described in *The Zero-Sum Society* a polity incapable of making tough decisions:

> Lacking a consensus on whose income ought to go down, or even the recognition that this is at the heart of the problem, we are paralyzed. . . . We wish to do something about our problems, but we endure them because we have not learned to play an economic game with a substantial zero-sum element. [15]

Indeed, at one level that entire book is a plea for strong leadership. We got strong leadership which knew how to impose loses. The result is greater inequality, just the opposite of what Thurow wanted. He has since admitted that he greatly overestimated the capacity of the poor to defend their interests. Yet there is a more general lesson to be learned here. Many a proposal stated too generally becomes available to those who would enact it in ways contrary to those which the originator intended.

Perhaps the central institutional arrangement which Thurow believes is essential to regaining U.S. competitiveness is some mechanism for directing investment. Just what

179

form this mechanism might take was not clear when he wrote in 1980. Such an investment bank could be a separate government agency or simply a cooperative arrangement among our current banks.[16] Since then, Thurow has developed a strong argument for a public investment bank in addition to private investment banks.[17] His main points are that a public bank can socialize risks which no single bank would undertake and can pursue broader social purposes rather than just short-term profits. In clarifying his position Thurow has stepped into the middle of a long-term debate between Michael Harrington and Felix Rohatyn.

First, let us be clear about what is at stake in this debate. Reich, Thurow, Rohatyn and Harrington all agree that they do not intend the sort of centralized bureaucratic planning practiced in the Soviet Union. Reich puts it this way:

> The answer is not "national planning," if we take that term to mean the centralized drafting of detailed blueprints for future economic management. We already have that sort of planning . . . within our giant corporations and government agencies. Instead, we need political institutions that are . . . versatile . . . less concerned with making "correct" decisions than with making correctable ones.[18]

Obviously, the practical problem is how to establish and preserve this flexibility. Thurow believes the market can help: "The goal is to set up a process in which government, labor, and management are encouraged to work together within a market framework to take actions to strengthen market outcomes. The state becomes not a central planner but a cooperative market player."[19] Looking for this same sort of give-and-take, Rohatyn refers to the procedures for developing this cooperation as "bargaining structures."[20] Harrington summarizes the danger they all fear in these terms: "Planning exercised by technocrats with a monopoly of the computers will obviously lead to some kind of authoritarian result. Of course, public bureaucracies are a threat to freedom as well as private bureaucracies."[21] All four,

180

then, are looking for some sort of dynamic negotiating process rather than a singular national planning agency.

Precisely at this point, Harrington argues against Rohatyn about just who should participate in that process and toward what ends. Harrington charges that in Rohatyn's scheme of things, corporate interests set the agenda, and an elite dominates the process. Rohatyn became famous as the man who negotiated, then administered the deal which saved New York City from bankruptcy. Harrington contends that the banks set the agenda, and the unions and city services were forced to meet their demands. The banks actually improved their financial standing under the arrangements negotiated. So much for the fair allocation of sacrifice which Rohatyn often claims is essential.

Applied to the economy at large, Harrington believes such an approach would result in government subsidies for corporations, the freezing or reduction of wages, and cutbacks in services to the disadvantaged. For Harrington, these results are inevitable, given Rohatyn's assumptions, which Harrington summarizes in this way:

> When corporations, and the corporate rich, are in charge of the critical investment decisions that determine the economic course of the society, they are, by that fact, more important than anyone else, including a democratic majority. Their prosperity is the key to the nation's prosperity, the source of investment funds; their decisions as to technology and plant location and pricing shape the future. Under such circumstances . . . government will *inevitably* discriminate in favor of the elite controlling basic allocations and choices.[22]

It is not enough, then, to argue for some sort of public investment. The question of power must be faced or the benefits of public involvement will naturally flow to those who now have power. Harrington's solution is consciously and consistently to democratize economic decisions. Certainly, any public authority set up to direct public investment is a good place to begin that process. Reich and Thurow would agree. Harrington's contribution, derived from years of thought and debate over appropriate forms of democratic planning, is to bring this issue to the center of the discussion.

All of these figures and the schools of thought they represent recognize the need for some forms of public planning. Lawrence and the traditional Keynesians want to limit that role to the macroeconomic context and to market failures. He and they are much more activist on both fronts than the various conservatives we have examined. Reich and Thurow agree with Lawrence, but see the need for greater government and guided investment. However, they retain a healthy respect for the market. Rohatyn and Harrington, in quite different ways, want broader forms of planning. Cutting across this continuum, as we have seen, is the question of who participates in, and whose interests are served by, this planning.

The Ethical Contribution

Thus far this discussion of options for the future has proceeded only in view of economic productivity. What we know from our previous ethical analysis is that these economic arguments also embody a moral argument with deep religious roots. What Thurow and Reich are doing when they raise questions about the myth of rugged individualism is affirming the very view of the human condition we developed in our theology of human action. Human beings are inherently related and communal. The Japanese seem to understand that much better than we do. Yet, more profoundly, Thurow and Reich are contending that human beings are more creative and productive when this related and communal side of what it means to be human is recognized.

It is in Harrington that we see the most consistent wrestling with what pluralistic community means in prac-tice. His sustained effort to explore all of the various dimensions of, and possible strategies for, developing a decentralized democratic planning process is in fact an attempt to delineate what pluralistic community would mean in actual economic and social policy. In our ethical terms, he is seeking a form of community pluralistic enough to preserve and support creative agency.

The policies advocated by these critics from the left may well lead to greater productivity. I believe they would. I am much more sure that they are infinitely more consistent with the basic religious insights we garnered from Whitehead and Arendt than the policies of the Reagan administration have been. They recognize that we humans are related to one another and are a part of common communities. Finally, they propose that our creativity as human beings has a greater chance of emerging when we act within the context of healthy relations and a dynamic, pluralistic community. Although that basic religious insight does not tell us with clarity just what policies we should enact, it does indicate that these critics of Reaganomics from the left are moving in the right direction ethically.

What they add to this ethical analysis is a sense of practical applicability. Often those of us who advocate policies aimed at bringing out the best in humans are patted on our heads for our noble principles and then dismissed as impossible idealists. At a more sophisticated level, the assumption that there is a trade-off between efficiency and equality and community or (speaking theologically) that we do not take sin seriously enough, lingers.[23] In the face of these criticisms, these economists offer economic data and interpretation that suggests that it is not only possible to pursue those ethical guidelines we have devised but may even be more productive economically.

Possibilities for Coalition

Yet, as we move back to the world of real possibilities and political compromise, these distinctions give way to coalition possibilities. Harrington concedes that "throughout the

183

foreseeable future, there will be private corporations with considerable economic power."[24] Thus, Harrington recognizes that for some time truly *democratic* socialists are going to find themselves advocating liberal capitalist reforms. This leads to criticism from some of his more radical fellow socialists. However, he has consistently insisted for all of the years of his public life that the only alternative to such compromise is political irrelevance. At the same time, Thurow includes Lawrence as one of the advocates of an industrial policy, because he does recognize that there are market failures which justify government intervention. What might all of these figures agree upon as a coalition agenda?

Let me suggest three broad areas of agreement related to the principles we have considered throughout our investigation. Specifically, these three proposals are based upon the self-transcendent understandings of liberty, equality, and solidarity which we developed from our theology of human action.

Liberty, Equality, and Community in Practice

If we are interested in liberty in terms of self-transcendence, it requires not that we be able to do what we want but that we be able to make a creative contribution. In a modern industrial world, this is increasingly difficult to do without education. Speaking only economically, high technology requires a labor force both skilled and flexible. This leads even the most conservative economists to emphasize the critical importance of human capital. When the political element is added, education becomes even more important. How can we expect to deal with all of the complex issues we have been considering in a democratic fashion without a well-educated citizenry? Education is key.

Yet American education is in trouble. The plain fact is that our work force is not as literate and technologically competent as our major economic competitors, and it seems

184

to be losing ground. Surely part of the reason is the accident of our history by which we ended up with our public schools largely dependent on local taxes set by local taxpayers. Imagine our military budget if the Pentagon had to pass local referenda every time they wanted a new weapons system. One result of this localism is a great disparity in the quality of our schools. We typically serve our students most in need of educational opportunity with our worst schools, and our students who start out with educational advantages with our best schools. The second result is that nearly all our schools are underfunded, and nearly all of our teachers are underpaid. Thus, many of our brightest and most capable potential teachers go elsewhere. Perhaps to compensate for this problem, educational bureaucracies have grown up in an effort to monitor and correct bad teaching. Sadly, they seem to harass and wear down good teachers in the process. The result is a demoralized profession from which a number of the most creative members burn out, while others hunker down into a boring routine. A visit to a public-school teachers' lounge is not usually an uplifting experience.

More ideas for reform of our educational system than can be reviewed here have appeared in recent years. Many of them hold promise for addressing part of the problem. It is hard to see how serious improvement will occur without major new investments. Given the realities of local electorates and the Federal deficit, state governments will have to carry much of that burden in the immediate future. In the meantime, there are millions of Americans who dropped out of school or graduated without an education. As Rohatyn puts it: "There are vast portions of our population that will never get the opportunity to compete for . . . jobs, because they will always be vocational and educational cripples."[25] Lawrence, Reich, Thurow, Rohatyn, and Harrington all agree that some form of expanded job training and employment program is needed. There is also now broad agreement with Thurow's thesis of nearly two decades ago that training without a job is inefficient. Thus, all propose

185

some sort of support for on-the-job training. Whether through tax breaks to employers, education and training vouchers for the unemployed, or guaranteed employment with training, we must begin to invest much more in human beings as well as plants and equipment.

Rightly or wrongly, it is hard for an able-bodied adult to be considered and to feel equal without a job. Certainly, a self-transcendent understanding of equality implies creative effort, not just equal incomes.[26] It is no accident that full employment is the natural rallying cry of the left. Again, all five of these men agree. Lawrence sees full employment as the central goal of good macroeconomic policy. It is hard to imagine any full employment program working outside of the context of fiscal and monetary policies which support solid and sustained economic growth. Reich would go further to support some job creation and training. Thurow and Harrington, as we saw much earlier, are closest to each other at this point. Both argue for various forms of public employment, both to guarantee jobs for workers, and also to force public officials to get their macroeconomic policy in order.

About the best the Reagan program could produce was 5 percent unemployment. Assuming with Rohatyn that "Reagan will ultimately be judged on his ability to put people to work,"[27] this was not a very good record. Any alternative to Reaganomics must move toward full employment. Such an effort is likely to require both the macroeconomic context Lawrence advocates, and the job training and job creation called for by Thurow and Harrington. Then a reformed welfare system can provide adequate assistance for those still without work. Without full employment, it is hard to imagine achieving the equality goal proposed by Thurow. It is certainly impossible to achieve that goal in a manner which embodies the kind of equality suggested by an emphasis on self-transcendence.

Every degree and form of public planning assumes community. Even when Lawrence proposes an agency to gather and analyze information about the effects of government intervention, he is recognizing that there is a public interest for which the government has responsibility. This recognition grows with Reich and Thurow, and especially with Rohatyn and Harrington. More and more in each case the needs of the community, as distinct from the interests of individuals, justify government involvement. The debate between Rohatyn and Harrington about the form of this public planning illustrates well our general discussion of community earlier. Harrington is much more attentive to the need for pluralism and participation than is Rohatyn. In our terms, he recognizes the claims of self-transcendent community much better.

In these various options to the left of Reagan is the possibility of a working coalition. At the policy level, such a coalition would emphasize the need to invest in human capital through improving our educational and job-training programs. Second, it would stress full employment through both better macroeconomic management and direct job creation. Finally, it would argue for various forms of democratic public planning as a way of marshaling resources, both human and financial, to produce economic growth. On the ethical level, such a coalition, at its best, would pull together an understanding of liberty that emphasizes creative contribution, an understanding of equality that supports and recognizes the contribution of each person, and an understanding of community that prizes pluralism and flexibility.

The 1988 campaign for the Presidential nomination of the Democratic Party indicated that a coalition in support of such policies is not just a theoretical construct. Every Democratic candidate for president stressed the need for greater development of human resources in general and larger investments in education in particular. All stressed full employment, and Paul Simon and Jesse Jackson in particular made it politically respectable to advocate direct job creation. Finally, all of them saw a need for greater government leadership in economic development through some sort of targeted investment. At this writing, I know neither who will win the nomination nor whether a Democrat or a Republican will be President of the United States. I do know that each of the policy directions which has emerged from this ethical analysis will be a part of our public debate. The more important question is whether a long-term political coalition in support of such policies can be forged.

We know well that actual societies, surely including our own, are composed of people who want theirs, want more than anyone else, and prefer a community composed only of people just like them. The question before us is whether such a policy can cope with the practical pressures of the present world economy, let alone hope to be a good society. There is, at least, the possibility that Robert Reich is correct when he says:

> The confidence that underpins cooperation depends on effective codes of fairness and on institutions that nurture a sense of economic citizenship—in short, on a potent concern with civic virtue. The notion that an atmosphere of civic membership and obligation is a requisite for prosperity may seem quaintly old-fashioned in an age of robots and micro-computers. But the logic is timeless: Civic virtue is not a matter of charity or ethics; it is the adhesive of social and economic life.[28]

Reich makes a convincing case that such economic citizenship is essential if we are to escape economic decline.

However, Reich is absolutely wrong about civic virtue and ethics. It is just the sort of civic virtue he describes that an ethical analysis of economics identifies as the appropriate ideal for a humane economy as we near the end of the twentieth century. This ideal does not dictate specific policy, but it does lure us to transcend our present economic structures toward more fully human embodiments of liberty, equality, and solidarity.

Notes

1. Lester Thurow, "Unexpected Wake Will Trail Recent Market Dive," *Los Angeles Times*, November 1, 1987, Part IV, p. 3.

2. Robert B. Reich, "Why Do We Care What Worries Wall Street?" *Washington Post National Weekly Edition*, December 21, 1987, p. 24.

3. Robert Z. Lawrence, *Can America Compete?* (Washington, D.C.: Brookings, 1984).

4. Ibid., p. 115.

5. Ibid., p. 116.

6. Ibid., pp. 134-37.

7. Ibid., p. 144.

8. Robert B. Reich, *The Next American Frontier* (New York: Penguin, 1983), is the best single source of his ideas.

9. Lester C. Thurow, *The Zero-Sum Solution* (New York: Simon and Schuster, 1985), pp. 95-102.

10. Ibid., p. 101.

11. Reich, *The Next American Frontier*, p. 20.

12. Thurow, *The Zero-Sum Solution*, pp. 122-23.

13. Ibid., p. 123.

14. Perhaps both can be traced back to feudal, if not tribal, roots as suggested in my discussion of the bishops' pastoral in chapter 7.

15. Lester C. Thurow, *The Zero-Sum Society* (New York: Basic Books, 1980), p. 25.

16. Ibid., p. 96.

17. Thurow, *The Zero-Sum Solution*, pp. 277-80.

18. Reich, *The Next American Frontier*, p. 277.

19. Thurow, *The Zero-Sum Solution*, p. 266.

20. Felix Rohatyn quoted in Jeremy Bernstein, "Profiles: Allocating Sacrifice," *The New Yorker* 58 (January 24, 1983): 77.

21. Michael Harrington, *Decade of Decision* (New York: Simon and Schuster, 1980), p. 325.

22. Michael Harrington, "A Path for America," *Dissent* 29 (Fall 1982): 416.

23. The classic statement of the conflict between equality and efficiency is Arthur Okun, *Equality and Efficiency: The Big Tradeoff* (Washington: Brookings Institution, 1975). The best statement of the sin argument is Robert Benne, *The Ethic of Democratic Capitalism: A Moral Reassessment* (Philadelphia: Fortress Press, 1981).

24. Harrington, "A Path for America," p. 417.

25. Rohatyn in Bernstein, "Profiles: Allocating Sacrifice," p. 74.

26. I developed this idea further in my discussion of welfare policy in Warren R. Copeland, "The Ethics of Welfare Reform," *The American Society of Christian Ethics, Selected Papers: 1978* (Newton Centre, Mass.: American Society of Christian Ethics, 1978), pp. 62-81.

27. Ibid., p. 78.

28. Reich, *The Next American Frontier*, p. 280.

Index